NATIONAL
ACADEMIES

Sciences
Engineering
Medicine

ONAL
DEMIES
S
ngton, DC

CW00385963

Aging in Place
with Dementia

Linda Casola, *Rapporteur*

Committee on Population

Board on Behavioral, Cognitive, and
Sensory Sciences

Division of Behavioral and Social
Sciences and Education

Proceedings of a Workshop

NATIONAL ACADEMIES PRESS 500 Fifth Street, NW Washington, DC 20001

This activity was supported by a contract between the National Academy of Sciences and the National Institute on Aging (HHSN263201800029I/ 75N98022F00008). Any opinions, findings, conclusions, or recommendations expressed in this publication do not necessarily reflect the views of any organization or agency that provided support for the project.

International Standard Book Number-13: 978-0-309-71372-6
International Standard Book Number-10: 0-309-71372-2
Digital Object Identifier: https://doi.org/10.17226/27420

This publication is available from the National Academies Press, 500 Fifth Street, NW, Keck 360, Washington, DC 20001; (800) 624-6242 or (202) 334-3313; http://www.nap.edu.

Suggested citation: National Academies of Sciences, Engineering, and Medicine. 2024. *Aging in Place with Dementia: Proceedings of a Workshop*. Washington, DC: The National Academies Press. https://doi.org/10.17226/27420.

The **National Academy of Sciences** was established in 1863 by an Act of Congress, signed by President Lincoln, as a private, nongovernmental institution to advise the nation on issues related to science and technology. Members are elected by their peers for outstanding contributions to research. Dr. Marcia McNutt is president.

The **National Academy of Engineering** was established in 1964 under the charter of the National Academy of Sciences to bring the practices of engineering to advising the nation. Members are elected by their peers for extraordinary contributions to engineering. Dr. John L. Anderson is president.

The **National Academy of Medicine** (formerly the Institute of Medicine) was established in 1970 under the charter of the National Academy of Sciences to advise the nation on medical and health issues. Members are elected by their peers for distinguished contributions to medicine and health. Dr. Victor J. Dzau is president.

The three Academies work together as the **National Academies of Sciences, Engineering, and Medicine** to provide independent, objective analysis and advice to the nation and conduct other activities to solve complex problems and inform public policy decisions. The National Academies also encourage education and research, recognize outstanding contributions to knowledge, and increase public understanding in matters of science, engineering, and medicine.

Learn more about the National Academies of Sciences, Engineering, and Medicine at **www.nationalacademies.org**.

Reviewers

This Proceedings of a Workshop was reviewed in draft form by individuals chosen for their diverse perspectives and technical expertise. The purpose of this independent review is to provide candid and critical comments that will assist the National Academies of Sciences, Engineering, and Medicine in making each published proceedings as sound as possible and to ensure that it meets the institutional standards for quality, objectivity, evidence, and responsiveness to the charge. The review comments and draft manuscript remain confidential to protect the integrity of the process.

We thank the following individual for their review of this proceedings:

LAURA N. GITLIN, Drexel University

Although the reviewer listed above provided many constructive comments and suggestions, they were not asked to endorse the content of the proceedings nor did they see the final draft before its release. We also thank staff member **TRACY LUSTIG** for reading and providing helpful comments on this manuscript.

The review of this proceedings was overseen by **JACQUI SMITH,** University of Michigan. She was responsible for making certain that an independent examination of this proceedings was carried out in accordance with standards of the National Academies and that all review comments were carefully considered. Responsibility for the final content rests entirely with the rapporteur and the National Academies.

Acknowledgments

Funding for the workshop was provided by the Division of Behavioral and Social Research of the National Institute on Aging (NIA), and NIA staff provided substantial input to the workshop. The planning committee thanks Elena Fazio, Nicole Kidwiler, Jessica Boten, and Priscilla Novak at NIA for being generous with their time and attention in answering the committee's questions and providing vital information to develop the scope and content of the workshop.

The planning committee is grateful to all the speakers for sharing their experiences and knowledge by providing high-quality and relevant presentations for this workshop. A video playlist of the workshop as well as links to all presentations can be found at: https://www.nationalacademies.org/event/40481_09-2023_aging-in-place-with-dementia-a-workshop. Finally, the workshop and proceedings would not be possible without help from knowledgeable and talented National Academies of Sciences, Engineering, and Medicine staff, who provided guidance, shared best practices, and assisted in navigating institutional processes and procedures.

This proceedings was prepared by the workshop rapporteur as a factual summary of what occurred at the workshop. The planning committee's role was limited to planning and convening the workshop. The views contained in the proceedings are those of individual participants and do not necessarily represent the views of all workshop participants, the planning committee, NIA, or the National Academies.

Contents

Box, Figures, and Tables

BOX

FIGURES

TABLES

1

Introduction

BACKGROUND

Many older adults would prefer to remain in their homes and communities as they age, but they may not understand or anticipate what support they will need and what resources are available to do so. "Aging in place" refers to "the ability to live in one's own home and community safely, independently, and comfortably, regardless of age, income, or ability level."[1] To age in place, individuals—especially those living with dementia—may need to plan for a variety of supports related to accessibility, health care, transportation, and social interaction.

Although much research has been conducted on community-level factors related to the risk of dementia in general, less is known about the factors that affect the ability of older adults with dementia to age in place successfully. Additional research could lead to a better understanding of the data and resources needed to support innovative approaches for adaptive housing,[2] services, and supports so that people living with dementia can remain in their communities.

Addressing the needs of communities where aging individuals are experiencing chronic illness, disability, and dementia is a complex, multidisciplinary task that requires partnerships across government, social service, public safety, urban planning, public health, and health systems. Several

---

[1] From the Centers for Disease Control and Prevention's Healthy Community Design Initiative: https://www.cdc.gov/healthyplaces/terminology.htm
[2] For an overview on adaptive or accessible housing see Cho et al., 2016.

countries have official "dementia-friendly" nongovernmental organizations, but research is limited on the design and policy features that make a community dementia friendly in the United States, as well as how these communities function to affect the health, well-being, and quality of life for people living with dementia and their care partners.

To discuss these needs and develop effective strategies for the future, the Committee on Population and Board on Behavioral, Cognitive, and Sensory Sciences of the National Academies of Sciences, Engineering, and Medicine (National Academies) convened a virtual workshop on aging in place with dementia on September 13–15, 2023. Sponsored by the National Institute on Aging (NIA), this workshop highlighted the state of knowledge and identified research gaps to inform conceptual approaches to guide research on dementia-friendly communities[3] in the U.S. context, building on existing approaches in the field. The workshop incorporated individual-level factors that enable aging in place, but it focused primarily on the structures in the community and neighborhood environments that influence the ability of residents with dementia to age in place: see Box 1-1 for the workshop's Statement of Task. Appendix A is the workshop agenda.

OPENING REMARKS

Workshop planning committee chair Emily Agree (Research Professor and Associate Director, Hopkins Population Center, Johns Hopkins University) welcomed participants to the workshop and described the workshop objectives: To discuss approaches that could be used to guide research and identify community- and neighborhood-level factors that enable aging in place for people living with dementia in the United States; to develop an agenda and establish priorities for future research and data collection, as well as strengthen the evidence base for policymakers; and to contribute to the efforts of broader communities of stakeholders and practitioners. She expressed her hope that this workshop would expand on the work presented in *Reducing the Impact of Dementia in America: A Decadal Survey of the Behavioral and Social Sciences* (National Academies of Sciences, Engineering, and Medicine, 2021).

Amy Kelley (NIA) noted that, as the workshop's sponsoring agency, NIA is committed to advancing research that helps adults, especially those living with dementia, to lead the lives they want to lead as they age in the communities of their choosing—where they have families, friends, and connections. She described research on aging in place as an NIA multiyear effort involving a broad range of community members and other partners.

---

[3] This concept has multiple usages that often vary by location. See Lin (2017) for a description.

BOX 1-1
Statement of Task

A planning committee of the National Academies of Sciences, Engineering, and Medicine will organize and execute a 2-day virtual public workshop that will bring together an interdisciplinary group of experts to discuss aging in place for people living with dementia in the United States. The workshop, which will draw on lessons and evidence from domestic and international research, will:

- Identify current research and future research needs on individual-level, structural, and environmental factors that should be considered in the development of programs supporting aging in place for people living with dementia.
- Discuss research approaches and needs to support aging in place of persons living with dementia (and their caregivers) from diverse racial, ethnic, and socioeconomic backgrounds and in different geographic contexts.
- Discuss components of existing conceptual models and measurements that can inform conceptual approaches for research on aging in place for people living with dementia.

After the workshop, a Proceedings of the Workshop summarizing the presentations and discussions at the workshop will be prepared by a designated rapporteur in accordance with institutional guidelines.

As this research effort continues, in part through this workshop, she underscored the importance of adopting a health equity lens. Many of her primary goals as NIA deputy director focus on improving health equity as well as better understanding and mitigating the lifelong health effects resulting from differences in social experiences and personal backgrounds. She emphasized that although aging in place may have significant social and emotional benefits for older adults, their care partners, and their communities, these benefits may be unequally distributed across communities and across the United States. Thus, she said, she championed the workshop planning committee's endeavor to help better understand the current state of knowledge on aging in place and to identify promising research paths.

Elena Fazio (Director of the Office of Alzheimer's Disease and Alzheimer's Disease-Related Dementias Strategic Coordination in the Division of Behavioral and Social Research [BSR] at NIA) elaborated on the workshop's relevance to NIA's strategic objectives. For example, in 2019, a review of BSR by its National Advisory Council on Aging recommended support for further research to improve care for people with dementia and their caregivers. Providing additional context for the workshop goals, she explained that 10% of adults aged 65 and older may develop dementia, and 22%[4] may have mild cognitive impairment (Manly et al., 2022). With the potential for so many people to be affected by dementia and related health challenges—many of whom wish to remain living in their own homes—creating a supportive plan to manage finances, make homes more accessible, meet health care needs, use transportation, and maintain social connections is critical to enable aging in place (see Crews et al., 2019; Liu et al., 2020; Szanton et al., 2011). She noted that NIA regularly receives inquiries about how older adults living with dementia can live healthy, safe, and supported lives *with dignity* in their own homes and/or communities.

In addition to these individual- and family-level considerations for people with dementia to age in place, Fazio mentioned challenges and opportunities at the community and state levels, such as the variation in services and supports needed; financial implications; the need for complex state- and community-level planning efforts; and recognizing diversity of experience, particularly that not everyone has equal access to supports. She reiterated that NIA is concerned about health equity and health care access. In addition, she said, to better inform future research efforts, NIA is interested in the perspectives of those who represent diverse racial, ethnic, and socioeconomic backgrounds and different geographic contexts as well as of those who live alone with dementia or mild cognitive impairment.

Fazio invited workshop speakers and participants to consider the following guiding questions to facilitate potential future research opportunities:

- How well do our models of the neighborhood and community factors that facilitate aging in place fit people living with dementia? What additional factors need to be taken into account? Are there unique challenges that differ from those of people with physical disabilities or chronic diseases? How do structural sources of disadvantage affect people living with dementia in these communities?
- What aspects of infrastructure affect the ability of people living with dementia to age in place? Can public spaces, transportation systems, and architecture be made more friendly for people living with dementia? Are there differences in urban and rural communities in the features that are most important to people living with dementia?
- To what extent should the goals of programs that support aging in place with dementia be targeted to keep people in their own homes versus in a community or social environment? Can aging in place for people living with dementia be evaluated in terms of improve-

---

[4]This number may be underestimated due to a lack of diagnoses, as discussed in Mattke et al. (2023).

ments in quality of life, deferring transitions to facility-based care, or other metrics?

- How can local health and social service systems be incorporated into community-level efforts to support people living with dementia, help them to stay in their own homes longer, and minimize adverse consequences? What is the role of physicians and other health care providers to improve quality of life and reduce hospitalization and institutionalization?
- How are people living with dementia vulnerable to risks of isolation? What individual- and community-level factors improve or worsen the consequences of isolation for people living with dementia? What interventions are available that might be useful to support those without family or friends?
- What research is needed to identify the challenges to implementation in real-world programs? Where is there room for innovations in delivery of services, organization of infrastructure, and supportive services? How can interventions be developed to be sustainable in diverse community settings?

ORGANIZATION OF THIS PROCEEDINGS

Chapter 2 offers commentary on existing frameworks for aging in place and how they could be adapted to incorporate people living with dementia. Chapter 3 describes how aspects of the built environment and community infrastructure affect that population. Chapter 4 considers strategies to measure and evaluate aging in place for people with dementia, and Chapter 5 focuses on the integration of social services and other supportive community resources. Chapter 6 explores issues of social isolation and engagement for that population. Finally, Chapter 7 highlights opportunities for future research to develop scalable interventions and new policies at the community level for people aging in place with dementia.

This proceedings has been prepared by the workshop rapporteur as a factual summary of what occurred at the workshop. The workshop planning committee's role was limited to organizing and convening the workshop: see Appendix B for biographical sketches of the workshop planning committee members and speakers. The views expressed in this proceedings are those of the individual workshop participants and do not necessarily represent the views of the participants as a whole, the planning committee, or the National Academies.

REFERENCES

Cho, H. Y., MacLachlan, M., Clarke, M., & Mannan, H. (2016). Accessible home environments for people with functional limitations: a systematic review. *International Journal of Environmental Research and Public Health, 13*(826), 1–24. https://doi.org/10.3390/ijerph13080826

Crews, D. C., Delaney, A. M., Walker Taylor, J. L., Cudjoe, T. K. M., Nkimbeng, M., Roberts, L., Savage, J., Evelyn-Gustave, A., Roth, J., Han, D., Lewis Boyér, L., Thorpe Jr, R. J., Roth, D. L., Gitlin, L. N., & Szanton, S. L. (2019). Pilot intervention addressing social support and functioning of low socioeconomic status older adults with ESRD: The Seniors Optimizing Community Integration to Advance Better Living with ESRD (SOCIABLE) Study. *Kidney Medicine, 1*(1), 13–20.

Lin, S. Y. (2017). Dementia-friendly communities' and being dementia friendly in healthcare settings. *Current Opinion in Psychiatry, 30*(2), 145–150.

Liu, M., Xue, Q. L., Samuel, L., Gitlin, L. N., Guralnik, J., Leff, B., & Szanton, S. L. (2020). Improvements of disability outcomes in CAPABLE older adults differ by financial strain status. *Journal of Applied Gerontology, 41*(2). https://doi.org/10.1177/0733464820975551

Manly, J. J., Jones, R. N., Langa, K. M., Ryan, L. H., Levine, D. A., McCammon, R., Heeringa, S. G., & Weir, D. (2022). Estimating the prevalence of dementia and mild cognitive impairment in the US: The 2016 Health and Retirement Study Harmonized Cognitive Assessment Protocol Project. *JAMA Neurology, 79*(12), 1242–1249.

Mattke, S., Jun, H., Chen, E., Liu, Y., Becker, A., & Wallick, C. (2023). Expected and diagnosed rates of mild cognitive impairment and dementia in the U.S. Medicare population: Observational analysis. *Alzheimer's Research & Therapy, 15*(128), 1–8.

National Academies of Sciences, Engineering, and Medicine. (2021). *Reducing the impact of dementia in America: A decadal survey of the behavioral and social sciences.* The National Academies Press.

Szanton, S. L., Thorpe, R. J., Boyd, C., Tanner, E. K., Leff, B., Agree, E., Xue, Q. L., Allen, J. K., Weiss, C., Seplaki, C. L., Guralnik, J. M., & Gitlin, L. N. (2011). CAPABLE: A bio-behavioral-environmental intervention to improve function and health-related quality of life of disabled, older adults. *Journal of the American Geriatrics Society, 59*(12), 2314–2320.

2

Frameworks for Aging in Place

Key Points Highlighted by Presenters

- Although people transitioning into dementia might experience a loss of agency and sense of belonging, as well as increased stigmatization and social exclusion, they can proactively co-create life spaces. Environmental stability; familiar surroundings; and possibilities to engage with people, places, and objects may foster continuity of self. **(OSWALD)**

- Structural determinants, including racism and social experiences, are critical to aging in place; what happens in the present was determined in the past. **(ADKINS-JACKSON)**

- Theories of age- and dementia-friendly initiatives implemented as complex interventions may help improve the health and well-being of people who are already aging in place. **(GREENFIELD)**

For the first session of the workshop, speakers examined how existing frameworks for aging in place could be adapted to incorporate people living with dementia. Speakers and workshop participants had been asked to explore the following questions: How well do models of the neighborhood and community factors that facilitate aging in place fit people who are living with dementia? What additional factors need to be taken into account? Are there unique challenges that differ from those of people with physical disabilities or chronic diseases? How do structural sources of disadvantage affect people living with dementia in their communities?

THEORIES OF PLACE AND AGING:
AN ENVIRONMENTAL GERONTOLOGY PERSPECTIVE

Frank Oswald (Professor of Interdisciplinary Aging Research, Goethe University, Frankfurt) discussed how, over the past few decades, home- and community-based environments have gained increased attention in the field of environmental gerontology. The process of theorizing place and aging includes (a) reconsidering "aging in place" and the "place of place" in the everyday lives of older adults, (b) identifying "enduring" and "novel" issues that have shaped theory on place and aging, and (c) exploring both traditional and more recent theoretical perspectives from environmental gerontology that provide context for further research on aging in place for people with dementia.

First, Oswald explained, the concept of "aging in place" indicates a person's desire and opportunity to remain in the home and live independently, with some assistance, for as long as possible without having to move to another place (Pani-Harreman et al., 2021). However, he noted, instead of using the phrase "aging in place," some scholars believe that "place" should be an overarching concept to address "aging" in the context of its many challenges, opportunities, and risks (for example, see Cutchin, 2018; Rhodus & Rowles, 2023; Rowles, 1993). This concept of "place" helps to understand how older adults are embedded in contexts, how they shape contexts, and how contexts influence the course of aging (for example, see Lewis & Buffel, 2020). Therefore, in addition to its importance at the micro-level, place relates to the meso- and macro-levels of neighborhood and community (for example, see Greenfield et al., 2019). As a result, he continued, place and aging interact and depend on historical development and cohort flow, and they are constantly changing in response to historical–cultural influences and transitions and global trends, such as digitalization or climate change.

Second, Oswald outlined the "enduring" perspectives of place: it may enhance or hinder access, orientation, and resource use at home, in the neighborhood, and in the community; it may support or constrain the experiences of privacy, comfort, recreation, social exchange, and community embeddedness; it may serve as a source of identity and meaning-making on different contextual layers; and it may provide the socio-physical frame for processes of continuous change over various time metrics. In addition, "novel" perspectives of place are shaped by ongoing megatrends (e.g., technology that enables or constrains place-making), increased diversity among older adults (e.g., ethnicity, cognitive status, lifestyle), and environmental and social innovations in community-based housing and support networks.

Third, Oswald noted, three generations of theories have conceptualized place and aging (Oswald et al., 2024). From the 1960s to the 1990s, many scholars viewed a person and the environment as independent entities. During this first generation of theory, research primarily focused on the physical dimension of the environment. From 2000 to 2015, the person and the environment were viewed instead as interwoven entities that influenced one another. New emphases on "agency" (i.e., becoming an agent in one's own life through intentional behaviors imposed on the socio-physical environment; for example, see Bandura, 2001, 2006) and "belonging" (i.e., non-goal-oriented cognitive and emotional process that makes a space a place; for example, see: Rowles, 1983; Rubinstein, 1987) emerged, and digitalization became a critical issue during this era of research. He remarked that current theoretical approaches have expanded this understanding of place to include more diverse contexts. Approaches in this third generation of theory include transactional and co-constructed perspectives on the interrelationship between person and place. New approaches are inspired by fields beyond environmental gerontology (e.g., human geography and material gerontology) that could influence future theory development as well as the application of interventions (e.g., Höppner & Urban, 2018; Rhodus & Rowles, 2023).

Oswald offered the following key takeaways from this review of theories of place and aging. New developments in the concept of place support the notion that people and environments are co-constitutive. Therefore, second- and third-generation theories are more appropriate than first-generation theories to address enduring and novel issues of place and aging in research and application. He added that differentiated measures have led to differentiated findings on the level of transaction (e.g., processes of agency and belonging) and on the level of participatory approaches (e.g., age-friendly communities). He advocated for a new focus on how people and places develop together or apart in a certain environment, instead of on what an age-friendly environment is and how place attachment[1] can be facilitated in later life.

Oswald next turned to a discussion of existing empirical evidence on person–environment exchange processes for people in the early stages of dementia. He described a scoping review based on a model of context dynamics in aging as a framework for aging in place for people with dementia (Niedoba & Oswald, 2023). This model categorized the study design and different environmental dimensions of individuals' life spaces, as well as the person–environment exchange processes of agency and belonging. He explained that 55% of the studies in the review used qualitative methods (e.g.,

---

[1]The term is explored in detail in Diener & Hagen (2022).

ethnography, photovoice); quantitative methods were used primarily to measure processes of agency (e.g., global positioning system assessments). Most of the studies prioritized the social and the physical environments, and only a few addressed care, technology, or socioeconomic factors.

Describing the review's evidence on the process of agency, Oswald indicated that people living with dementia can deliberately reduce, maintain, use, or expand their life spaces. Although people in the early stages of dementia often experience a "shrinking world" (Duggan et al., 2008), with reduced global movement (Tung et al., 2014) and increased mobility restriction (Wettstein et al., 2015), the extent to which places are visited depends on their type and meaning. For example, consumer, administrative, and self-care places, as well as social, cultural, and spiritual places and places for recreational and physical activities, are visited less often than they used to be; places with contact with nature, for medical care, for staying in touch with their social network, and the neighborhood continue to be visited (Margot-Cattin, 2021). Therefore, according to Ward et al. (2021), even after being socially excluded, people living with dementia can rebuild their social networks, strengthen existing relationships, and find spaces where they can establish new social contacts.

Describing the review's evidence on the process of belonging, Oswald commented that people living with dementia still perceive connectedness and familiarity with the socio-physical environment, although a feeling of belonging may decrease. Studies indicate a persistent desire for belonging (for example, see Han et al., 2016; Mattos, 2016) and the promotion of community belonging through participation in social groups (for example, see Söderhamn et al., 2014), as well as perceived familiarity and safety at home (for example, see Duggan et al., 2008; van Gennip et al., 2016), to reinforce continuity of one's sense of self and identity (Margot-Cattin, 2021). Besides the home (Li et al., 2019), objects (Dooley et al., 2021) and, interestingly, clothing can also support identity (Buse & Twigg, 2016), especially in the early stages of dementia. As dementia progresses, visits to relatively new current places may become unfamiliar and less important than visits to known past places (Duggan et al., 2008; Genoe, 2009; Pace, 2020). According to van Wijngaarden et al. (2019, p. 14): "Gradually, the world becomes an increasingly alien place. The feeling of basic familiarity diminishes. Meaningful connections between the self and the outside space are interrupted, creating feelings of not-being-at-home and insecurity."

Oswald shared the following key takeaways from this review of evidence on person–environment exchange processes. He noted that "place" plays a significant role in either enabling or impeding the transition into dementia. Although people making this transition may experience a loss of agency and sense of belonging, stigmatization, and social exclusion, they are not victims of their environments because they can co-create life spaces proactively. He underscored that environmental stability; familiar surroundings; and possibilities to engage with people, places, and objects might foster continuity of one's feeling of self despite this progression of dementia. Because current findings are limited to a traditional framework on distinct physical and social environments and conventional concepts of person–environment exchange processes (for example, see Oswald & Wahl, 2019), he suggested directing more attention toward new theories as well as studying both places outside one's home (for example, see Sugiyama et al., 2022) and the technological environment (for example, see Gaugler, 2023).

STRUCTURAL DETERMINANTS OF AGING IN A PLACE: A STORY

"AJ" Adkins-Jackson (Assistant Professor of Epidemiology and Sociomedical Sciences, Columbia University) provided an overview of the relationship between social and structural determinants and aging in place, inspired by the lived experience of her grandmother, Helen Musick. Following Gómez et al. (2021), Adkins-Jackson defined social determinants as the conditions in the environments where people are born, live, learn, work, play, worship, seek health care, and age.

Reflecting first on the social determinant of education, Adkins-Jackson noted that Helen, born in 1930, attended an integrated elementary school in Syracuse, New York, and pointed out that much of the discussion surrounding the social determinant of education focuses on the relationship between education and future cognitive ability. She cited a report that suggested that addressing disparities in access to education early in life might reduce the risk factor for dementia prevalence by 7% (Livingston et al., 2020). However, she said, the issue is far more complex: education does not necessarily provide cognitive exposure, especially for today's older adults of color who experienced pain and trauma as schools became desegregated. Although the evidence is mixed on the benefits of integrated education in particular, she underscored that education provides access to future occupations and income that then influence one's ability to have a good quality of life and the potential to age in place.

Although Helen attended an integrated school, she lived in a segregated neighborhood, the borders of which were policed. Thus, Adkins-Jackson explained, where a person lives is another critical social determinant. She asserted that communities deprived of resources were (and are) located across from thriving communities by design, not by happenstance. For example, she shared a 1937 map of Syracuse that displayed highways built directly through Black neighborhoods, causing extensive disruption and displacement.

Moving to Los Angeles in 1949, Helen encountered similar community segregation. She married and found work cleaning homes and caring for children of White families located 10 miles from her own neighborhood.

Adkins-Jackson indicated that where a person works is another key social determinant. For instance, the workplace might expose employees to toxins that could affect physical and cognitive abilities later in life. However, she explained, most of the dementia research focuses on the relationship between work and cognitive stimulation. Labor-intensive jobs are thought to be less cognitively stimulating than "desk jobs," yet, in reality, using both the body and the mind for work is incredibly cognitively stimulating. She described this as an example of how people and their work are devalued across generations and added that society often underestimates the role that work plays in people's potential to age in place. For instance, often only full-time employment provides the health insurance and financial stability required to enable a good quality of life. According to the National Partnership for Women and Families (2023), Black women are at a particular disadvantage, making only 64 cents to the dollar in comparison with White men, and their quality of life is directly and negatively affected by this wage theft.

In addition to the distance Helen had to travel for work, she had to ride a bus to take her children to the park because her neighborhood did not have one. Adkins-Jackson highlighted that this social determinant—where a person plays—is influenced significantly by the notions of both "choice" and "access." She explained that structural policies, such as eminent domain, allow governments to take property from residents and convert it for public use. For instance, Central Park, where people now play, was constructed after the predominantly Black Seneca Village residents were forced to leave in 1857 and their homes were subsequently torn down.

With consideration for this historical context, Adkins-Jackson transitioned from the discussion of social determinants to a discussion about structural determinants—which she defined as the pervasiveness and deliberateness with which policies, societal norms and structures, and governing processes result in inequities in the distribution of power, resources, opportunities, and social determinants of health (Gómez et al., 2021; Crear-Perry et al., 2021): also see Figure 2-1.

Adkins-Jackson commented on several structural determinants that merit additional research, including homophobia, ageism, ableism, capitalism and other socioeconomic biases, religious biases, xenophobia and other geographic biases, structural sexism and genderism, and structural racism and other ethnocultural biases—all of which determine a person's quality and quantity of life (Adkins-Jackson et al., 2023). In particular, structural racism operates by grouping individuals on the basis of categories of perceived similarities; groups are then assigned value through a ranking system; and racism structures opportunity and dictates how people within the system treat others. With particular attention toward the structural violence that many Black communities have endured, she asserted that structural racism determines who has the opportunity to age—and to age

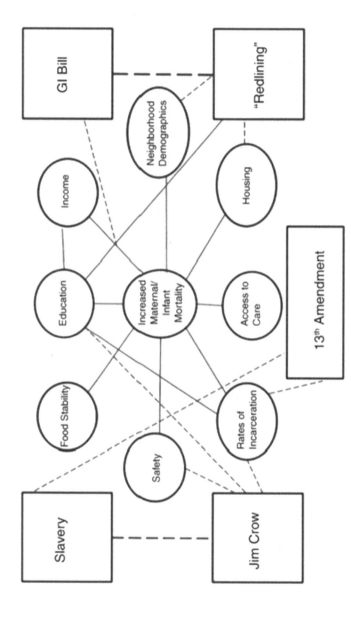

FIGURE 2-1 The impact of structural determinants on social determinants of health.
NOTE: Boxes connected by dashed line = structural determinants; circles and solid lines = distribution of social determinants
SOURCE: Roach (2016). Reprinted with permission.

in place. Health thus becomes a commodity in a discriminatory system, she continued; people try to survive, but the system causes them to die in place (Gee et al., 2019). Furthermore, this exposure to racism occurs across the life course reflected in, among other things, certain anticrime bills, intergenerational poverty, racist encounters with medical professionals, and accumulating pollution in communities (Glymour & Manly, 2008).

Resuming the story of her grandmother, Adkins-Jackson noted that the concept of aging in place is complicated; tragically, some people are *surviving* in place because they are unable to plan for aging and thus unable to age in place. Where one is surviving in place dictates where that person receives care. For example, Helen, who is now experiencing dementia, commutes 10 miles outside of her community to receive health care, and her health concerns are often dismissed in these predominantly White care settings. Adkins-Jackson explained that Helen's experiences with residential segregation; displacement; pollution; occupational segregation; wage theft; and challenges related to food, health care, transportation, and access to social supports created this situation of "surviving in place." She underscored that this "aging in (dis)placement" has occurred for hundreds of years and continues through the multigenerational determinants that prevent people from accessing the resources that would allow them to age *well* in place.

In closing, Adkins-Jackson asserted that structural determinants, structural racism, and social determinants are critical to the notion of aging in place; what happens in the present was determined in the past, and our elders who have endured such disparities deserve to age how and where they choose.

FRAMEWORKS FOR AGE- AND DEMENTIA-FRIENDLY COMMUNITY INITIATIVES

Emily Greenfield (Professor of Social Work and Director of the Hub for Aging Collaboration, Rutgers University) opened her presentation with a discussion of conceptualizing communities as a social unit for aging and dementia. She said that communities are defined broadly as connections across a set of people through a combination of shared beliefs, circumstances, priorities, relationships, or concerns, typically formalized through institutions at the local level, such as faith-based and civic groups (Chaskin, 1997). In aging research in particular, communities are often thought to be formed by people with shared social identities who connect across space and time through digital technologies; around specific organizations, such as churches, senior centers, and residential housing settings; or geographically—that is, where they live, work, or play.

Greenfield explained that communities are one of the many contexts in which aging individuals are embedded. Therefore, conceptual models often place individuals at the center. However, she indicated, theorizing about aging extends beyond the role of the individual, as researchers may be more interested in theorizing on and changing the communities in which individuals live. As a result, a new conceptual framework for community gerontology situates communities in the meso-level context, interacting with micro-level social dynamics and macro-level social contexts (Greenfield et al., 2019). She asserted that adopting this perspective offers new insights into developing frameworks for interventions, as well as into systematically changing micro-level social interactions to improve communities for aging with dementia.

Greenfield underscored that this understanding of how communities both affect people and are affected by people contrasts historical representations of communities by aging and health researchers, in which communities were often described as settings to receive services and as external forces acting on people (e.g., social determinants of health). Instead, she advocated for community-centered approaches to health and aging, especially for people aging with dementia. Community-based social innovations for aging and community-centered approaches to public health view communities as both a target of and an engine for change (South, 2015; Yasumoto & Gondo, 2021). For example, Public Health England's community-centered approaches to public health concentrate on enhancing a community's capacity to change social determinants of health, tapping community members' networks and information channels for health, encouraging multisectoral collaboration on health, and facilitating civic engagement as a means for health (South, 2015). Although not specifically described as community-centered approaches to aging, she noted that several U.S. programs—such as Memory Cafes,[2] Naturally Occurring Retirement Communities,[3] the Village to Village Network,[4] and other age- and dementia-friendly community initiatives—exemplify the principles of these approaches.

Greenfield next turned to a discussion of advancing frameworks specifically for age- and dementia-friendly community initiatives. She noted that the World Health Organization initially developed the concept of age-friendly communities more than 20 years ago by creating a framework of eight characteristics encompassing social, built, and service environments that make cities amenable to aging.[5] Public-sector involvement is centered at the subnational level to advance these age-friendly communities. In the United States, the age-friendly national network is supported by American

---

[2] https://www.memorycafedirectory.com
[3] https://aging.ny.gov/naturally-occurring-retirement-community-norc
[4] https://www.vtvnetwork.org
[5] The 8 characteristics are: Community and health care; transportation; housing; social participation; outdoor spaces and buildings; respect and social inclusion; civic participation and employment; as well as communication and information.

Association of Retired Persons (AARP). The concept of dementia-friendly communities first emerged in Japan in 2005, she explained, expanded to the United Kingdom, and began in the United States in the early 2010s—specifically, in Minnesota. Dementia Friendly America,[6] a national network of dementia-friendly community efforts supported by USAging, emerged in 2015. She explained that dementia-friendly communities highlight strategies to make local communities more responsive to aging in place for people with dementia, focus broadly on inclusion of and supports for people living with dementia and their care partners, improve design and service of physical infrastructure, and reduce the stigma around aging with dementia.

Greenfield emphasized that age- and dementia-friendly community efforts have developed separately but in parallel. Both initiatives prioritize multisector collaboration across public, private, civic, and academic stakeholders; the joining of place-based communities with global, national, state, and regional networks; and social planning models that convene multisector groups to conduct participatory community assessments, create action plans, implement those plans, and measure progress in meeting goals (Rémillard-Boilard et al., 2020; Scher & Greenfield, 2023). If age- and dementia-friendly initiatives are to serve as interventions for aging in place for people with dementia, she continued, such interventions have to be theorized as complex interventions (Hawe, 2015). She underscored that such interventions help improve the health and well-being of people who are already aging in place (Thomas & Blanchard, 2009). For example, Scharlach (2017) describes "constructive aging" as involving six interrelated processes: continuity, compensation, control, connection, contribution, and challenge. Greenfield noted that these developmental outcomes are of greatest relevance when theorizing about the population health significance of age- and dementia-friendly community initiatives.

Before concluding her presentation, Greenfield highlighted opportunities for research. She remarked that researchers and research funders with a shared vision play an important role across sectors to improve community contexts for aging in place for people with dementia. Research can serve as a tool to:

- help move from programmatic initiatives to community interventions,
- optimize the roles of people with lived experience involved in the work to drive community change, and
- motivate consortiums to support (a) the people in communities who are doing the work, (b) learning and action networks for community leaders, and (c) science for impact, equity, sustainability, and scalability.

---

[6] See https://www.dfamerica.org

DISCUSSION

Sharing questions from workshop participants, the session chair, Jennifer Manly (Professor of Neuropsychology at Columbia University; planning committee member) moderated a discussion among the session's three speakers. She asked how dichotomies among people and places—for example, mentally healthy versus cognitively impaired people, or residential setting versus nursing home settings—limit the effectiveness of research.

Oswald replied that researchers in some academic disciplines are more comfortable with poststructuralist thought than others, but he encouraged all researchers to overcome their biases and develop creative new solutions by viewing dementia as a transition. Adkins-Jackson remarked that more voices that represent lived experiences need to be included in the research canon. She also cautioned that diversifying disciplines of study does not automatically result in diverse perspectives. Greenfield added that because current methods are limited in their capacity to honor the complexity of people's lived experiences, researchers should be humble. As one strategy to address this level of complexity, she advocated for communities to become the units of analysis. Manly observed that dementia experiences differ for each person, which further complicates efforts to understand aging in place for people with dementia.

Elena Fazio (Director of the Office of Alzheimer's Disease and Alzheimer's Disease-Related Dementias Strategic Coordination, Division of Behavioral and Social Research, National Institute on Aging) asked how well existing frameworks of neighborhood and community factors that facilitate aging in place fit for people with dementia. Oswald argued that as processes of individuals' agency decrease over time later in life, processes of belonging might increase. However, this assumption does not apply for people with cognitive impairment or dementia, which creates additional challenges.

Expanding on the discussion of strategies to conduct more effective research, Manly inquired about how people with dementia are included in the conduct, analysis, and presentation of research. Greenfield remarked that she and her team are learning how to do this incrementally and thoughtfully. They recently reviewed a case study of participatory approaches in research on Alzheimer's disease and related dementias and concluded that much variety exists in how researchers are including people with lived experience: few clear norms on how that information should be reported have emerged. She advocated for more transparent processes in publications as well as greater clarity and intentionality in the language used and in the limitations of participatory studies, which could result in a more just and more rigorous use of participatory methods for research.

Adkins-Jackson referenced Andrea Gilmore-Bykovskyi (Gilmore-Bykovskyi et al., 2022), who has published suggestions on how to conduct participatory research, and Northwestern University, which has a mentorship program that pairs a medical student with a person living with dementia. Adkins-Jackson also highlighted the value of providing background information to, having conversations with, and seeking feedback from not only the person with dementia but also the family and caregivers—and obtaining consent from all—when conducting research.

Oswald referenced several relevant studies, including an interdisciplinary study on how to guarantee informed consent processes when engaging people with dementia in research (Haberstroh & Müller, 2017). He also described a study that provides empirical evidence on the best environment for people to receive a dementia diagnosis (Florack et al., 2023), as well as a study about a program in Frankfurt that draws on and expands a program at the Museum of Modern Art in New York that offers a course for people with dementia and their relatives that included museum visits and workshops to maintain and promote social participation and a sense of belonging to the community (Adams et al., 2022).

Terri Lewinson (Associate Professor, Dartmouth Institute for Health Policy and Clinical Practice) wondered how to encourage people of color to trust the health care system, seek medical care, and be involved in medical research after years of historical wrongs committed against the Black community. Adkins-Jackson suggested offering reparations and restorative justice to initiate healing and serve as a step to mend the relationship before asking people to participate in research.

A workshop participant posed a question about how technology can enable place-making processes in the digitalized world. Greenfield said she expected an increased focus on the use of new technologies to address long-standing issues. For example, the state of New York used public funds to purchase approximately 70,000 voice-operated smart technology devices for people aging in place who are at risk for isolation and loneliness. She underscored the need for cross-disciplinary efforts to develop and evaluate such approaches that could accelerate social change.

Oswald explained that as digitalization continues to expand in Germany, the divide continues to grow between younger generations who are online and older generations who are not. He noted that digitalization affects daily social exchange processes, such as voting or reading a newspaper. Referencing Adkins-Jackson's presentation, he added that one's biography, history, and lived experience affect one's use of technology, especially later in life. Therefore, he said, leveraging technology solutions to enable people to age in place is complex owing to issues of barriers and access. Adkins-Jackson added that technology often exacerbates existing disparities and inequities, and she advocated for emerging technology efforts to focus on equity at the start of innovation.[7]

REFERENCES

Adams, A-K., Oswald, F., & Pantel, J. (Hrsg.) (2022). *Museumsangebote für Menschen mit Demenz. Ein Praxishandbuch zur Förderung kultureller und sozialer Teilhabe*. Kohlhammer.

Adkins-Jackson, P. B., George, K. M., Besser, L. M., Hyun, J., Lamar, M., Hill-Jarrett, T. G., Bubu, O. M., Flatt, J. D., Heyn, P. C., Cicero, E. C., Zarina Kraal, A., Pushpalata Zanwar, P., Peterson, R., Kim, B., Turner 2nd, R. W., Viswanathan, J., Kulick, E. R., Zuelsdorff, M., Stites, S. D., . . . Babulal, G. (2023). The structural and social determinants of Alzheimer's disease related dementias. *Alzheimer's & Dementia, 19*(7), 3171–3185. https://doi.org/10.1002/alz.13027

Bandura, A. (2001). Social cognitive theory: An agentic perspective. *Annual Reviews of Psychology, 52*, 1–26.

___. (2006). Toward a psychology of human agency. *Perspectives on Psychological Science, 1*(2), 164–180.

Buse, C., & Twigg, J. (2016). Materializing memories: Exploring the stories of people with dementia through dress. *Ageing and Society, 36*(6), 1115–1135.

Chaskin, R. J. (1997). Perspectives on neighborhood and community: A review of the literature. *Social Service Review, 71*(4), 521–547. http://www.jstor.org/stable/30012640

Crear-Perry, J., Correa-de-Araujo, R., Lewis Johnson, T., McLemore, M. R., Neilson, E., & Wallace, M. (2021). Social and structural determinants of health inequities in maternal health. *Journal of Women's Health, 30*(2), 230–235. https://doi.org/10.1089/jwh.2020.8882

Cutchin, M. P. (2018). Active relationships of aging people and places. In M. W. Skinner, G. J. Andrews, & M. P. Cutchin (Eds.), *Geographical gerontology: Perspectives, concepts, approaches* (pp. 216–228). Routledge.

Diener, A. C., & Hagen, J. (2022) The power of place in place attachment, *Geographical Review, 112*(1), 1–5.

Dooley, J., Webb, J., James, R., Davis, H., & Read, S. (2021). Everyday experiences of post-diagnosis life with dementia: A co-produced photography study. *Dementia, 20*(6).

Duggan, S., Blackman, T., Martyr, A., & Schaik, P. V. (2008). The impact of early dementia on outdoor life: A "shrinking world"? *Dementia, 7*(2).

Florack, J., Abele, C., Baisch, S., Forstmeier, S., Garmann, D., Grond, M., Hornke, I., Karakaya, T., Karneboge, J., Knopf, B., Lindl, G., Müller, T., Oswald, F., Pfeiffer, N., Prvulovic, D., Poth, A., Reif, A., Schmidtmann, I., Theile-Schürholz, A. Ullrich H., & Haberstroh, J. (2023). Project DECIDE, part II: Decision-making places for people with dementia in Alzheimer's disease: Supporting advance decision-making by improving person-environment fit. *BMC Medical Ethics, 24*(26). https://doi.org/10.1186/s12910-023-00905-0

Gaugler, J. E. (2023). Introductory editorial: Cultivating the formidable legacy of the gerontologist. *The Gerontologist, 63*(1), 1–2. https://doi.org/10.1093/geront/gnac166

Gee, G. C., Hing, A., Mohammed, S., Tabor, D. C., & Williams, D. R. (2019). Racism and the life course: Taking time seriously. *American Journal of Public Health, 109*(S1), S43–S47. https://doi.org/10.2105/AJPH.2018.304766

Genoe, M. R. (2009). *Living with hope in the midst of change: The meaning of leisure within the context of dementia*. UWSpace. http://hdl.handle.net/10012/4500

---

[7]See the end of Chapter 3 for a summary of this session and the following one.

Gilmore-Bykovskyi, A., Croff, R., Glover, C. M., Jackson, J. D., Resendez, J., Perez, A., Zu-elsdorff, M., Green-Harris, G., & Manly, J. J. (2022). Traversing the aging research and health equity divide: Toward intersectional frameworks of research justice and participation. *The Gerontologist, 62*(5), 711–720. https://doi.org/10.1093/geront/gnab107

Glymour, M. M., & Manly, J. J. (2008). Lifecourse social conditions and racial and ethnic patterns of cognitive aging. *Neuropsychology Review, 18*, 223–254. https://doi.org/10.1007/s11065-008-9064-z

Gómez, C. A., Kleinman, D. V., Pronk, N., Wrenn Gordon, G. L., Ochiai, E., Blakey, C., Johnson, A., & Brewer, K. H. (2021). Addressing health equity and social determinants of health through Healthy People 2030. *Journal of Public Health Management and Practice, 27*(Suppl 6), S249–S257. https://doi.org/10.1097/PHH.0000000000001297

Greenfield, E. A., Black, K., Buffel, T., & Yeh, J. (2019). Community gerontology: A framework for research, policy, and practice. *The Gerontologist, 59*(5), 803–810.

Haberstroh J., & Müller T. (2017). Einwilligungsfähigkeit bei Demenz: Interdisziplinäre Perspektiven. *Zeitschrift für Gerontologie und Geriatrie, 50*(4), 298–303. https://doi.org/10.1007/s00391-017-1243-1

Han, A., Radel, J., McDowd, J. M., & Sabata, D. (2016). Perspectives of people with dementia about meaningful activities: A synthesis. *American Journal of Alzheimer's Disease and Other Dementias, 31*(2), 115–123. https://doi.org/10.1177/1533317515598857

Hawe, P. (2015). Lessons from complex interventions to improve health. *Annual Review of Public Health, 18*(36), 307–323. https://doi.org/10.1146/annurev-publhealth-031912-114421

Höppner, G., & Urban, M. (Eds.). (2019). Materialities of age and ageing: Concepts of a material gerontology. *Frontiers in Sociology.* https://doi.org/10.3389/978-2-88945-863-9

Lewis, C., & Buffel, T. (2020). Aging in place and the places of aging: A longitudinal study. *Journal of Aging Studies, 54*, 100870.

Li, X., Keady, J., & Ward, R. (2019). Transforming lived places into the connected neighbourhood: A longitudinal narrative study of five couples where one partner has an early diagnosis of dementia. *Ageing and Society, 13*, 1–23. https://doi.org/10.1017/S0144686X1900117X

Livingston, G., Huntley, J., Sommerlad, A., Ames, D., Ballard, C., Banerjee, S., Brayne, C., Burns, A., Cohen-Mansfield, J., Cooper, C., Costafreda, S. G., Dias, A., Fox, N., Gitlin, L. N., Howard, R., Kales, H. C., Kivimäki, M., Larson, E. B., Ogunniyi, A., . . . Mukadam, N. (2020). Dementia prevention, intervention, and care: 2020 report of the Lancet Commission. *Lancet, 396*(10248), 413446. https://doi.org/10.1016/S0140-6736(20)30367-6

Margot-Cattin, I. (2021). *Participation in everyday occupations and situations outside home for older adults living with and without dementia: Paces, familiarity and risks* [Doctoral dissertation, Karolinska Institutet]. ProQuest Dissertations Publishing.

Mattos, M. K. (2016). *Mild cognitive impairment in older, rural-dwelling adults* [Doctoral dissertation, University of Pittsburg]. ProQuest Information & Learning. https://core.ac.uk/download/pdf/78482992.pdf

National Partnership for Women & Families. (2023). *Quantifying America's gender wage gap by race/ethnicity fact sheet.* https://nationalpartnership.org/wp-content/uploads/2023/02/quantifying-americas-gender-wage-gap.pdf

Niedoba, S., & Oswald, F. (2023). Person-environment exchange processes in transition into dementia: A scoping review. *The Gerontologist.* https://doi.org/10.1093/geront/gnad034

Oswald, F., & Wahl, H.-W. (2019). Physical contexts and behavioral aging. *Oxford research encyclopedia of psychology.* Oxford University Press. https://doi.org/10.1093/acrefore/9780190236557.013.399

Oswald, F., Wahl, H.-W., Wanka, A., & Chaudhury, H. (2024). Theorizing place and aging: Enduring and novel issues in environmental gerontology. In M. P. Cutchin & G. D. Rowles (Eds.), *Handbook of aging and place*. Edward Elgar Publishing.

Pace, J. (2020). "Place-ing" dementia prevention and care in NunatuKavut, Labrador. *Canadian Journal on Aging*, 39(2, SI), 247–262. https://doi.org/10.1017/S0714980819000576

Pani-Harreman, K. E., Bours, G. J. J. W., Zander, I., Kempen, G. I. J. M., & van Duren, J. M. A. (2021). Definitions, key themes, and aspects of "ageing in place": A scoping review. *Ageing & Society*, 41(9), 2026–2059.

Rémillard-Boilard, S., Buffel, T., & Phillipson, C. (2020). Developing age-friendly cities and communities: Eleven case studies from around the world. *International Journal of Environmental Research and Public Health*, 18(1), 133. https://doi.org/10.3390/ijerph18010133

Rhodus, E. K., & Rowles, G. D. (2023). Being in place: Toward a situational perspective on care. *The Gerontologist*, 63(1), 3–12.

Roach, J. (2016). *ROOTT's theoretical framework of the web of causation between structural and social determinants of health and wellness—2016*. Restoring Our Own Through Transformation. https://www.roottrj.org/web-causation

Rowles, G. D. (1983). Geographical dimensions of social support in rural Appalachia. In G. D. Rowles & R. J. Ohta (Eds.), *Aging and milieu: Environmental perspectives on growing old* (pp. 111–129). Academic Press.

Rowles, G. D. (1993). Evolving images of place in aging and "aging in place." *Generations: Journal of the American Society on Aging*, 17(2), 65–70.

Rubinstein, R. L. (1987). The significance of personal objects to older people. *Journal of Aging Studies*, 1, 225–238.

Scharlach, A. E. (2017). Aging in context: Individual and environmental pathways to age-friendly communities. *The Gerontologist*, 57(4), 606–618. https://doi.org/10.1093/geront/gnx017

Scher, C. J., & Greenfield, E. A. (2023). Variation in implementing dementia-friendly community initiatives: Advancing theory for social change. *Geriatrics*, 8(2), 45. https://doi.org/10.3390/geriatrics8020045

Söderhamn, U., Aasgaard, L., & Landmark, B. (2014). Attending an activity center: Positive experiences of a group of home-dwelling persons with early-stage dementia. *Clinical Interventions in Aging*, 9, 1923–1931.

South, J. (2015). *A guide to community-centered approaches for health and wellbeing*. Public Health England. https://eprints.leedsbeckett.ac.uk/id/eprint/1229

Sugiyama, M., Chau, H.-W., Abe, T., Kato, Y., Jamei, E., Veeroja, P., Mori, K., & Sugiyama, T. (2022). Third places for older adults' social engagement: A scoping review and research agenda. *The Gerontologist*, 63(7), 1149–1161. https://doi.org/10.1093/geront/gnac180

Thomas, W. H., & Blanchard, J. M. (2009). Moving beyond place: Aging in community. *Generations*, 33(2), 12–17.

Tung, J. Y., Rose, R. V., Gammada, E., Lam, I., Roy, E. A., Black, A. E., & Poupart, P. (2014). Measuring life space in older adults with mild-to-moderate Alzheimer's disease using mobile phone GPS. *Gerontology*, 60(2), 154–162.

van Gennip, I. E., Pasman, H. R. W., Oosterveld-Vlug, M. G., Willems, D. L., & Onwuteaka-Philipsen, B. D. (2016). How dementia affects personal dignity: A qualitative study on the perspective of individuals with mild to moderate dementia. *Journals of Gerontology Series B Psychological Sciences & Social Sciences*, 71(3), 491–501.

van Wijngaarden, E., Alma, M., & The, A.-M. (2019). "The eyes of others" are what really matters: The experience of living with dementia from an insider perspective. *PLoS One*. https://doi.org/10.1371/journal.pone.0214724

Ward, R., Rummery, K., Odzakovic, E., Manji, K., Kullberg, A., Keady, J., Clark, A., & Campbell, S. (2021). Beyond the shrinking world: Dementia, localisation and neighbourhood. *Ageing and Society, 42*(12), 2892–2913. https://doi.org/10.1017/S0144686X21000350

Wettstein, M., Wahl, H.-W., Shoval, N., Auslander, G., Oswald, F., & Heinik, J. (2015). Identifying mobility types in cognitively heterogeneous older adults based on GPS-tracking: What discriminates best? *Journal of Applied Gerontology, 34*(8), 1001–1027.

Yasumoto, S., & Gondo, Y. (2021). CBSI as a social innovation to promote the health of older people in Japan. *International Journal of Environmental Research and Public Health, 18,* 4970. https://doi.org/3390/ijerph18094970

3

Community-Level Built Environments and Infrastructure

Key Points Highlighted by Presenters

- Cognability is a theory of how supportive an area is to cognitive health through built and social environmental features that encourage physical activity, social connection, and cognitive stimulation in later life. (**FINLAY**)

- Balancing the desire to meet the physical and emotional needs of older people with the need to avoid physical and emotional harms is challenging but critical for decision making related to driving and aging in place. (**BETZ**)

- The residential stress model explores how one's perception of residence helps understand whether that person's environment is healthy or unhealthy as well as highlights coping strategies that residents leverage to improve their housing experiences and their overall well-being. (**LEWINSON**)

During the second session of the workshop, speakers had been asked to discuss how aspects of the built environment and community infrastructure affect aging in place for people with dementia by considering the following questions: What aspects of infrastructure affect the ability of people living with dementia to age in place? Can public spaces, transportation systems, and architecture be made more friendly for people living with dementia? Are there differences in urban and rural communities in the features that are most important to people living with dementia?

COGNABILITY: AN ECOLOGICAL THEORY OF NEIGHBORHOODS AND COGNITIVE AGING

Jessica Finlay (Assistant Professor of Geography, University of Colorado Boulder) explained that while studying aging in place experiences among racially and socioeconomically diverse older adults she learned that being diagnosed with Alzheimer's disease or a related dementia was one of people's greatest fears. Referencing the synthesis by Livingston et al. (2020) on how factors across the life course may theoretically prevent or delay dementia, she highlighted the specific role of built and social environments in affecting these risk factors.

Finlay and a team at the University of Michigan created the cognability project to study this connection between neighborhoods and dementia risk. They coined the term "cognability," which they initially defined as a theory of how supportive an area is to cognitive health through built and social environmental features that encourage physical activity, social connection, and cognitive stimulation in later life: for example, public libraries, educational programs, visual landmarks, coffee shops, shaded benches, well-designed crosswalks, traffic calming, mixed-use design, and public green spaces. To identify specific neighborhood features that may support healthy cognitive aging, Finlay and her team used a mixed-methods approach. Qualitative data collection and analysis helped understand where and how older adults socialize, exercise, and engage in cognitively stimulating activities outside of their homes; quantitative data collection and analysis helped determine how the availability of and access to these neighborhood sites are associated with cognitive function.

Finlay first provided an overview of the qualitative data collection. As part of the Aging in the Right Place (AIRP) study, 125 interviews were conducted with older adults from 2015 to 2016 in 3 demographically and geographically varied areas of Minneapolis to learn about their neighborhood experiences and their perceptions of necessary supports for aging in place. The average age of the interview participants was 71.3 years; 67% identified as female and 33% as male; 57% identified as White, 25% identified as Black, and 18% self-identified as other races and ethnicities; 34% identified as married and 66% as not married; 33% were living alone;

and 57% had a high school education and 43% had some postsecondary education (Finlay & Bowman, 2017). To capture a broader set of experiences and places, Finlay also conducted an ethnography with a subset of 6 participants over 12 months.

Finlay next presented an overview of the quantitative data collection, which leveraged the Reasons for Geographic and Racial Differences in Stroke (REGARDS) study. Ongoing since 2003, the REGARDS study includes more than 30,000 non-Hispanic Black and White adults. Annual follow-up with participants includes cognitive testing, residential address tracking, and physical and mental health measurement. She explained that multiple sources of information from the REGARDS study—for example, tests for language and executive function, learning and memory, and recall and orientation—were used to develop a global measure of cognition. The quantitative sample included 21,151 participants, limited to those in urban and suburban areas to align with the sample in the AIRP study. The average age of the REGARDS sample at assessment was 67 years; 56% identified as female and 44% as male; 60% identified as White and 40% as Black; and 60% had a high school education and 40% had some postsecondary education. Interestingly, cognition varied widely depending on where the person lived.

Finlay emphasized that the AIRP study was used for a qualitative thematic analysis to understand how and why participants perceived and used their local environments. The REGARDS study was used for a quantitative analysis using multilevel linear regression models and generalized additive models to measure global cognitive function and neighborhood features (with consideration for kernel density, individual buffers, and census tracts) among participants active 2006–2017, adjusted for individual- and area-level covariates.

Findlay explained that these qualitative and quantitative analyses were used to create pathways to build the concept of cognability. The qualitative analysis revealed that places for social connection and support among older adults included senior centers, civic and social organizations, and food and drinking establishments that were physically and economically accessible and often walkable destinations (Finlay, Esposito, Li, Kobayashi, et al., 2021). The quantitative analysis revealed that civic and social organizations and senior centers were positively associated with cognitive function. Although she noted that this exploratory work primarily uncovered correlations, it also helped to determine that social connection is one of the pathways to cognability.

To establish another pathway to cognability in relation to physical activity, Finlay and her team found, through the qualitative analysis, that places for active aging included walkable destinations, local parks, and recreation centers (Finlay, Esposito, Li, Colabianchi, et al., 2021). The quantitative analysis suggested that walkable destinations, parks, and recreation centers were all positively associated with cognitive function. She noted that the influences of cognitive stimulation through arts and cultural sites, as well as the hazards from highways and pollution sites, were also explored to better understand the full concept of cognability (Finlay, Yu, et al., 2021; Yu et al., 2023): see Figure 3-1.

Finlay indicated that all of these findings about the connections between neighborhood and cognitive health can be combined to create a whole-neighborhood model (Finlay et al., 2022). First, the quantitative analysis revealed that civic and social organizations had a strong positive association with better health outcomes. Positive associations were also identified for the arts, museums, and recreation centers. Highways had a strong negative association with cognitive health, and coffee shops and fast food establishments had a negative association with cognitive function. Second, Finlay and her team considered whether neighborhood features were more or less important to different subpopulations given that structural racism, sexism, and classism could make sites less accessible and thus less beneficial for some people. She explained that, although allowing the full set of neighborhood drivers of cognitive function to vary by race, gender, and education did not yield substantial improvements to the full model, some individual neighborhood features differed significantly by group. For example, religious organization density was significantly and positively associated with cognitive health among Black adults (Taylor et al., 2017). As this work continues in the future, Finlay described an opportunity for theoretically motivated and targeted investigations.

In closing, Finlay emphasized that much work remains to refine the concept of cognability. She and her team developed a website that maps cognability scores by location,[1] which may help determine where to target limited resources to bolster neighborhoods more equitably. Next steps include validating and extending the concept of cognability with nationally representative samples, as well as advancing understanding of earlier life environments and exposures, gene–environment interactions, rural communities, international contexts, and perceived social environments and expectations. Because COVID-19 significantly changed neighborhood landscapes and aging in place, she noted that mixed methods analyses are under way to develop "cognability 2.0."

DRIVING AND AGING IN PLACE: EMOTIONS, MOBILITY, AND TECHNOLOGY

Emmy Betz (Professor of Emergency Medicine, University of Colorado School of Medicine) highlighted the need to develop strategies to address difficult topics in a more supportive way as people age. She described a

---

[1] https://cognability.isr.umich.edu

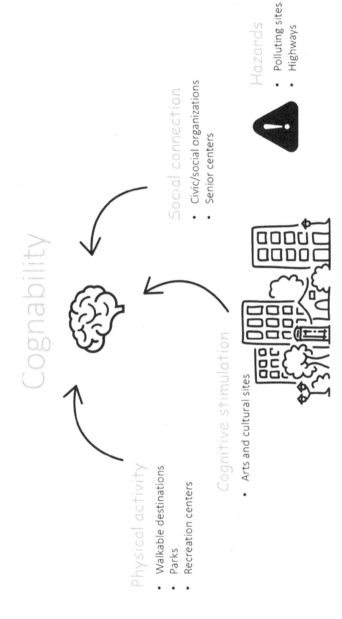

FIGURE 3-1 Pathways to cognability.
SOURCE: Adapted from Finlay, Yu, et al. (2021); Yu et al. (2023).

study on how people make decisions about the appropriate time to stop driving, noting that people's needs change over time, and most people outlive their ability to drive safely by approximately 10 years (Foley et al., 2002). Many older adults without cognitive impairment can recognize sight and other deficits and may restrict themselves from driving at night, driving long distances, or driving in bad weather; some may simply choose not to drive as their lifestyles change. However, other older adults, especially those in rural communities or those without reliable public transit, have a practical need for transportation and thus continue to drive. Furthermore, for some older adults, the act of driving symbolizes an important sense of freedom. Therefore, she cautioned against making assumptions about people's needs as they age.

Betz noted that while these aspects of physical and mental health may make continuing to drive important, associated risks also exist. For example, driving is a way to maintain social engagement and avoid isolation, but physical conditions can affect driving ability. She emphasized that balancing the physical and mental health needs of older adults with the physical and mental health needs and financial and logistical issues of family members (who may be called on to transport them or, conversely, need their assistance in transporting grandchildren) is critical. This interrelationship between older adults and their families is complicated, and not all older adults have a family structure surrounding them.

Betz indicated that communities play a key role in preserving safety, reducing stigma, distributing resources equitably, and maintaining engagement for older adults. Elaborating on the issue of stigma against older drivers and road safety, she noted that driver injury and death rates increase with age; however, because older adults are more likely to drive slower, less likely to drive at night, and less likely to drive impaired than younger drivers, the predominant risk to pedestrians is from younger drivers. She explained that location is also key to understanding the risks and resources for older adults who drive, as well as to making decisions about when to stop driving (Payyanadan et al., 2018). For example, those who live in cities can have their groceries delivered, which means that driving is not needed for essential tasks. Those who live in rural areas may need to keep driving to meet their daily needs; however, because rural areas are less densely populated, residents have less chance of hurting someone while driving.

Betz reiterated that meeting the physical and emotional needs of older people (e.g., going to religious services, to the doctor, to the grocery store) and avoiding physical and emotional harms (either from vehicle accidents or from negative health outcomes that may result in stopping a person's freedom to drive) is a challenge. Cognitive impairment in particular is a serious risk for driving, so she encouraged normalizing conversations about "driving health" by engaging people in planning for and decision making about the future before significant impairment develops and harm results (Betz et al., 2013, 2016). She noted that caregiver perspectives are particularly important in this space.

Betz proposed that some of these difficult issues could be addressed by designing interventions that are person centered and that leverage technology to meet the varied needs of older adults. She presented a transtheoretical model in relation to driving, in which adults move from thinking about the issue when mobility remains unchanged, to recognizing when mobility begins to change, to preparing with reduced driving, to stopping driving and maintaining mobility in other ways (Meuser et al., 2013). Factors that affect this journey include cognitive ability, attitudes, and social circumstances. She noted that work is under way to understand how a decision aid could help with this decision-making process. For instance, she and her team conducted a randomized controlled trial that leveraged this transtheoretical model with older adults who are currently driving but have a medical condition that may compel them to stop driving in the next few years. Results of the trial indicated that the decision aid reduced ambivalence, decreased decisional conflict, and increased knowledge about decisions to stop driving (Betz, Hill, et al., 2022).

Betz explained that this randomized controlled trial also revealed that older adults' experiences during COVID-19 provided important insights about the potential for and benefits of virtual engagement. For example, Betz, Fowler, et al. (2022) noted that 70% of older people reduced their driving during COVID-19 for a variety of reasons compared with only 26% before COVID-19. Furthermore, despite the increased social isolation of COVID-19, increased depression and stress were not observed among the older adults in this study.[2] Some learned how to use Zoom for social connection and realized that they could survive by driving less, while others drove just to escape the confines of their homes, thus reinforcing the complexity of people's psychological relationship with driving and the challenges of decision making about driving.

Moving forward, Betz advocated for the use of technology to enable increased alternative transportation options (e.g., Uber Central or Lyft's Lively Senior Ride Service, which caretakers can use to schedule rides for older people who may have difficulty navigating the platforms), as well as for efforts to make these alternatives financially feasible. She noted, however, that additional alternatives *to* transportation are needed—for example, online religious services, grocery delivery, and telehealth appointments. In closing, Betz mentioned that work is ongoing to create plans for safe mobility among older adults; she encouraged workshop participants to read *Transportation and Aging: An Updated Research Agenda to Advance Safe*

---

[2] Betz indicated that the cohort was comprised of educated and socioeconomically wealthy adults.

Mobility among Older Adults Transitioning from Driving to Non-driving (Dickerson et al., 2019).

AGING IN PLACE WITH DEMENTIA-FRIENDLY HOUSING

Terri Lewinson (Associate Professor, Dartmouth Institute for Health Policy and Clinical Practice) began her presentation by sharing words from Dolores Hayden: "Whoever speaks of housing must also speak of home; the word means both the physical space and the nurturing that takes place there" (Hayden, 1984, p. 63). Lewinson noted that when discussing housing plans and policies, people often lose focus of these social and communal experiences that occur in the physical space of the home. The dynamic psychosocial constructs that influence whether one calls a "house" a "home" include shelter and protection, autonomy and privacy, warmth, personalization and self-identity, aesthetics, continuity (i.e., patterned behaviors), and centrality (i.e., where you return at the end of every day and are welcomed). She asserted that many of these constructs may be disrupted or difficult to achieve in an institutional setting, in public housing, or when transitioning to a new place.

Lewinson explained that one's "perception of residence" helps understand whether a person's environment is healthy or unhealthy. The residential stress model, an environment–behavior model for residential settings (see Bell et al., 2001), can be leveraged to help understand these perceptions, which are influenced by the design of the residence; by the person's role(s) in community, family, and social groups; and by the ability of the residence to meet the person's needs: see Figure 3-2.

For those who are "precariously housed," often in extended-stay hotels and on the verge of homelessness, Lewinson noted that this model illuminates numerous mental health stressors—such as fear and confusion about the potential harm from transient neighbors and of systems that could initiate eviction; social isolation and loneliness owing to broken networks and troubled family histories related to abuse or nonacceptance of identity; and anxiety and depression over environment-related health losses, financial depletion, and temporal housing "in-betweenness." She emphasized that these mental health stressors combine with social and physical stressors to compound housing stressors; however, this model also highlights possible coping strategies that people can leverage to improve their housing experiences and thus their overall well-being.

Lewinson remarked that the housing and health disparities conceptual model (Swope & Hernandez, 2019), which identifies structural oppressions that keep people in precarious housing, is another valuable tool to help understand the relationship between housing and health. For example, it identifies how people lose financial and health equity throughout their

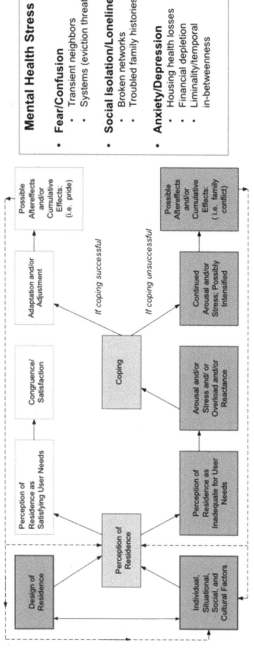

FIGURE 3-2 Residential stress model.
SOURCE: Adapted from Bell et al. (2001, pp. 402–403).

lives. Because 39% of extremely low–income renters are older people, she indicated that aging in place for people who are precariously housed is incredibly difficult because of a lack of resources. She highlighted current research funded by the National Institute on Aging that explores how people experience their homes and some of the stressors they confront and address. In particular, this research considers the role of resident service coordinators in supporting aging in place with the inclusion of dementia-friendly programming.

With consideration of these challenges related to the relationship between housing and health that impacts one's ability to age in place, Lewinson presented the key necessities for aging in place and dementia-friendly planning: (a) safe, accessible, and affordable housing; (b) community support services that are integrated and accessible; (c) accessible health care and crisis intervention; (d) transportation; (e) safety measures; (f) social and recreational opportunities; (g) caregiver support; (h) legal and financial support; (i) technology and communication; (j) collective advocacy and policy support; as well as (k) dementia-friendly spaces and resources, including sensory-friendly environments and recreational facilities, parks, and activities.

DISCUSSION

Sharing questions from workshop participants, Wendy Rogers (Khan Professor of Applied Health Sciences, University of Illinois Urbana-Champaign; planning committee member), moderated a discussion among the session's three speakers. She highlighted several themes that emerged across their presentations: the value of person-centric approaches, problematic issues of ageism and related stigma, variance in individual issues across older people, and the potentially helpful role of technology.

Rogers asked the speakers to identify key issues in urban versus rural settings related to the study of older people with dementia. Finlay replied that neighborhood measurement should change to accommodate rural and urban contexts. Although the types of community organizations in rural and urban areas may be very different, she noted that commonalities also exist that support aging in place in any setting. Betz added that the differences between urban and rural settings are also influenced by the type of place in which older adults live—for example, in a multigenerational home with caregivers or in a home alone. Furthermore, she stressed that the exploration of older adults' experiences is important; rural areas have many strengths owing to their tight-knit communities, but both urban and rural areas have several unique positive and negative features related to aging in place with dementia. Lewinson commented that resources may be restricted or unavailable in rural areas. She also explained that in both rural and urban areas, providing coordinated services is essential, and existing local relationships and frameworks are important for building engagement and support for people living with dementia. For example, she said that simple signage helps older people navigate their communities, and diverse housing design helps enable aging in place—but the United States is lagging in its housing offerings for people living with dementia and their caregivers.

Workshop planning committee member Sarah Szanton (Dean and Patricia M. Davidson Health Equity and Social Justice Endowed Professor, Johns Hopkins University) mentioned that Carehaus,[3] located in Baltimore and Houston, creates buildings of housing units both for people with and without dementia and for their direct care workers and their families. Over time, these direct care workers receive equity in the building in addition to their wages. She described this as a promising model of creating new "third spaces" for older people with dementia. Lewinson cited another model, Hotel Louisville[4] in Kentucky, which integrates social service agencies in the same buildings where precariously housed people live.

Szanton remarked that structural racism across the life course influences how activity spaces are used, as many people may feel like these spaces were not built for them. Finlay observed that using geography as a measure of access is inadequate—for example, a local park with a confederate statue is not accessible to all neighborhood residents, despite its proximity. Issues related to ableism also arise for spaces that are difficult for people to navigate. She advocated for the increased use of mixed methods research to begin to expand access, equity, and justice, especially for underserved communities.

Rogers posed a question to Finlay about variance *within* neighborhoods and another question about whether scent sensitivity has been explored as an explanation of why people do not frequent certain places. Finlay replied first that understanding variance within neighborhoods is difficult with quantitative research; qualitative research is more valuable. For example, while conducting interviews, she found that people who lived next door to each other reported completely different experiences of the same environment. Second, she said, that although limited research exists related to the sense of smell, there is much more research on auditory experiences and innovations in soundscapes because many locations are too loud for older people.

Rogers then asked Lewinson whether research has been conducted on the role of pets in aging in place for people with dementia. Lewinson replied that studies of residents in assisted living places found that pets help calm residents and improve their socialization with other residents. She described this as an interesting area for future research.

---

[3] https://www.carehaus.net
[4] https://hotellouisville.org/about-us

Rogers inquired about other certifications, training, or frameworks to guide people in age-inclusive design. Lewinson highlighted the notion of green design and encouraged the creation of more aesthetic spaces where older people can engage with nature and their senses. Betz expressed her hope that vehicle designers would begin to consider the needs of older adults and those with visual or physical challenges as they design new vehicle technology (e.g., simplified touchscreens and navigation tools).

Finlay pointed to work in the field of environmental gerontology, such as implementing different colored doors and noise-reduction strategies, to help older people navigate complex settings. She suggested building on successful training in occupational therapy to help people with cognitive impairment develop strategies to navigate new environments. She also noted that there are effective models for facilitating connections and care for older adults who might not yet be identified as vulnerable. For example, postal workers in the United Kingdom were trained to chat with isolated older adults on their route as a way to check-in, build community, and provide support if needed. Szanton encouraged an increased focus both in research and in practice on engaging older adults with dementia who live by themselves—which is approximately one-third of people with dementia. Some of these adults do not have caregivers or a support network, and they are often excluded from research because they are more socially isolated and thus more difficult to enroll in studies.

Rogers asked Betz about issues of technology acceptance among older adults with dementia and strategies to ensure the availability of instructional support. Betz responded that research is under way to explore the uptake and value of various vehicle technology features: For example, some evidence supports the benefits of passive interventions, such as automatic braking capabilities (Eby et al., 2018). However, the effectiveness of other features, such as flashing lights in sideview mirrors to warn of blind spots, remains in question. She added that financial equity is a critical dimension of any discussion about technology interventions, because not everyone can afford to buy a new car with these or other features. She noted that there is a study among older drivers that showed significant variance in technology readiness, and she underscored that instructional support is essential for the success of any technology intervention, as is developing strategies to embed support resources instead of making people find the resources themselves.

SUMMARY OF WORKSHOP DAY 1

Planning committee chair Emily Agree (Research Professor and Associate Director, Hopkins Population Center, Johns Hopkins University) summarized her key takeaways from the first two sessions of the workshop. Speakers discussed frameworks and conceptual models for thinking about aging in place for people with dementia. Several speakers indicated that the concept of place varies (e.g., geographically, virtually, by community type) and should be considered broadly, not only as a diverse context in which people live, but also as an interactive space that evolves in tandem with the way people live their lives. Furthermore, the preference to age in place is not universal. For instance, some older adults are "stuck" in place as they age and unable to improve their environments because of lifelong exposure to structural discrimination and disadvantages.

Agree noted that several speakers had discussed the way researchers approach this work. For example, the community plays a critical role in supporting people with dementia, and these ideas about community can be translated into programs in diverse communities. Working with existing community groups and leaders is essential to implement interventions in the real world. Additionally, several speakers had discussed the role that the built and community-level environment plays for aging in place for people with dementia—including such "third spaces" as senior centers, parks, and recreation centers outside the home—in maintaining cognitive health and improving well-being. However, different communities experience different benefits from different institutions. She noted that several speakers asserted that exploring the physical barriers that might hinder access to those spaces is essential.

Agree highlighted that one speaker had discussed the central role that driving plays in U.S. culture and identity. Decision aids could be helpful to reduce stress and conflict within families over this issue and to make decisions about stopping driving more acceptable to older people as they move into their next stage of life. Alternatives to driving would also be beneficial, as would forming alliances with new stakeholders to promote livable and age- and dementia-friendly communities with transportation options. Finally, some speakers had described the meaning of home and how housing instability and residential insecurity exacerbate problems for people aging with dementia. Strategies to provide safe and affordable housing as well as community support services are needed, especially for those who are the most vulnerable because of their earlier life experiences and current situations.

REFERENCES

Bell, P. A., Greene, T. C., Fisher, J. D., & Baum, A. (2001). *Environmental psychology* (5th ed.). Harcourt Publishers.

Betz, M. E., Fowler, N. R., Duke Han, S., Hill, L. L., Johnson, R. L., Meador, L., Omeragic, F., Peterson, R. A., & DiGuiseppi, C. (2022). Impact of the COVID-19 pandemic on older adult driving in the United States. *Journal of Applied Gerontology, 41*(8), 1821–1830.

Betz, M. E., Hill, L. L., Fowler, N. R., DiGuiseppi, C., Duke Han, S., Johnson, R. L., Meador, L., Omeragic, F., Peterson, R. A., & Matlock, D. D. (2022). "Is it time to stop driving?": A randomized clinical trial of an online decision aid for older drivers. *Journal of the American Geriatrics Society, 70*(7), 1987–1996.

Betz, M. E., Jones, J., Petroff, E., & Schwartz, R. (2013). "I wish we could normalize driving health": A qualitative study of clinician discussions with older drivers. *Journal of General Internal Medicine, 28*(12), 1573–1580.

Betz, M. E., Scott, K., Jones, J., & DiGuiseppi, C. (2016). "Are you still driving?": Metasynthesis of patient preferences for communication with health care providers. *Traffic Injury Prevention, 17*(4), 367–373.

Dickerson, A. E., Molnar, L. J., Bédard, M., Eby, D. W., Berg-Weger, M., Choi, M., Grigg, J., Horowitz, A., Meuser, T., Myers, A., O'Connor, M., & Silverstein, N. M. (2019). Transportation and aging: An updated research agenda to advance safe mobility among older adults transitioning from driving to non-driving. *Gerontologist, 59*(2), 215–221.

Eby, D. W., Molnar, L. J., Zakrajsek, J. S., Ryan, L. H., Zanier, N., Louis, R. M. S., Stanciu, S. C., LeBlanc, D., Kostyniuk, L. P., Smith, J., Yung, R., Nyquist, L., DiGuiseppi, C., Li, G., Mielenz, T. J., Strogatz, D., & LongROAD Research Team. (2018). Prevalence, attitudes, and knowledge of in-vehicle technologies and vehicle adaptations among older drivers. *Accident Analysis & Prevention, 113*, 54–62. https://doi.org/10.1016/j.aap.2018.01.022

Finlay, J. M., & Bowman, J. A. (2017). Geographies on the move: A practical and theoretical approach to the mobile interview. *The Professional Geographer, 69*(2), 263–274.

Finlay, J., Esposito, M., Langa, K. M., Judd, S., & Clarke, P. (2022). Cognability: An ecological theory of neighborhoods and cognitive aging. *Social Science & Medicine, 309*, 115220.

Finlay, J., Esposito, M., Li, M., Colabianchi, N., Zhou, H., Judd, S., & Clarke, P. (2021). Neighborhood active aging infrastructure and cognitive health: A mixed-methods study of aging Americans. *Preventive Medicine, 150*, 106669.

Finlay, J., Esposito, M., Li, M., Kobayashi, L. C., Khan, A. M., Gomez-Lopez, I., Melendez, R., Colabianchi, N., Judd, S., & Clarke, P. J. (2021). Can neighborhood social infrastructure modify cognitive function? A mixed-methods study of urban-dwelling aging Americans. *Journal of Aging and Health, 33*(9), 772–785.

Finlay, J., Yu, W., Clarke, P., Li, M., Judd, S., & Esposito, M. (2021). Neighborhood cognitive amenities? A mixed-methods study of intellectually-stimulating infrastructure and cognitive function among older Americans. *Wellbeing, Space & Society, 2*, 100040.

Foley, D. J., Heimovitz, H. K., Guralnik, J. M., & Brock, D. B. (2002). Driving life expectancy of persons aged 70 years and older in the United States. *American Journal of Public Health, 92*(8), 1284–1289.

Hayden, D. (1984). *Redesigning the American dream: The future of housing, work, and family life.* W. W. Norton & Co.

Livingston, G., Huntley, J., Sommerlad, A., Ames, D., Ballard, C., Banerjee, S., Brayne, C., Burns, A., Cohen-Mansfield, J., Cooper, C., Costafreda, S. G., Dias, A., Fox, N., Gitlin, L. N., Howard, R., Kales, H. C., Kivimäki, M., Larson, E. B., Ogunniyi, A., . . . Mukadam, N. (2020). Dementia prevention, intervention, and care: 2020 report of the Lancet Commission. *Lancet, 396*(10248), 413446. https://doi.org/10.1016/S0140-6736(20)30367-6

Meuser, T. M., Berg-Weger, M., Chibnall, J. T., Harmon, A. C., & Stowe, J. N. (2013). Assessment of Readiness for Mobility Transition (ARMT): A tool for mobility transition counseling with older adults. *Journal of Applied Gerontology, 32*(4), 484–507.

Payyanadan, R. P., Lee, J. D., & Grepo, L. C. (2018). Challenges for older drivers in urban, suburban, and rural settings. *Geriatrics (Basel), 3*(2), 14.

Swope, C. B., & Hernandez, D. (2019). Housing as a determinant of health equity: A conceptual model. *Social Science & Medicine, 243*, 112571.

Taylor, R. J., Chatters, L. M., Lincoln, K., & Woodward, A. T. (2017). Church-based exchanges of informal social support among African Americans. *Race and Social Problems, 9*(1), 53–62.

Yu, W., Esposito, M., Li, M., Clarke, P., Judd, S., & Finlay, J. (2023). Neighborhood "disamenities": Local barriers and cognitive function among Black and White aging adults. *BMC Public Health, 23*(1), 197.

4

Evaluating Successful Programs

Key Points Highlighted by Presenters

- Most effective programs that target individuals or caregivers are multicomponent (combining counseling, support, education, stress, mood, management, and skills training) and are tailored to specific needs. However, no one program is effective for all desired outcomes, and because samples tend to underrepresent diversity in terms of race, culture, language, ethnicity, and geography, which group's benefit most remains unclear. (**GITLIN**)

- Successful research about and practice of aging in place is complicated by a lack of coordination and collaboration across the housing, social service, and health care sectors, as well as a lack of integration of housing data and health data. (**MOLINSKY**)

- Little is known about the short- and long-term health benefits of and resource implications for age-friendly communities, but some studies suggest that aging-well interventions generate a positive social return on investment; the next step is to explore how that information can be used to support program implementation efforts. (**LAFORTUNE**)

For the third session of the workshop, speakers explored how to measure and evaluate programs and other interventions for people with dementia aging in place. Speakers and workshop participants had been asked
to consider the following questions: To what extent should the goals of
programs that support aging in place with dementia be targeted to keep
people in their own homes versus in a community or social environment
that might better suit their needs? Can aging in place for people living with
dementia be evaluated in terms of improvements in quality of life, deferred
transitions to facility-based care, or other metrics?

AN INTERVENTIONIST'S PERSPECTIVE

Laura Gitlin (Distinguished Professor and Dean Emeritus, College of
Nursing and Health Professions, Drexel University) asserted that comprehensive dementia care is needed to support people aging in the *right*
place, and she presented a socio-ecological model for guiding appropriate
interventions (Gitlin & Hodgson, 2018). Constructing these multilevel,
complex interventions to enable aging in the right place and to improve
well-being requires consideration of individual-level neurobiological, behavioral, health, and social factors; an understanding of the "right place" in
relation to how it affects family members and other caregivers; awareness
of different kinds of living environments and related issues of accessibility,
safety, maintenance, and stimulation; consideration of community-level
services and supports; participation of health and human services systems
(including Medicaid-funded home- and community-based services and adult
day services); and implementation of national policies: see Figure 4-1.

Gitlin indicated that because dementia is a progressive disease, a person's
needs will change with each new stage. Thus, the right place for aging may
change as the disease progresses, which creates additional challenges. She
emphasized that this concept of aging in place has not been well defined
in the past 50 years of dementia care research, which primarily developed
interventions to address the clinical symptoms of dementia, as well as more
than 200 types of interventions to provide support, knowledge, and strategies
to family caregivers. However, she noted, the emerging research considers more
complex interventions through a health equity lens. Instead of only targeting
individuals and their caregivers, these interventions help create a knowledgeable
workforce in community-based services (e.g., at the agency level and for home
modifications) to better support those individuals and their families.

Gitlin shared the following lessons learned from hundreds of clinical
trials targeting individuals or caregivers, which could be useful as the next
generation of interventions is designed:

- Supportive programs for caregivers are highly effective at addressing psychosocial outcomes, but evidence of the effectiveness

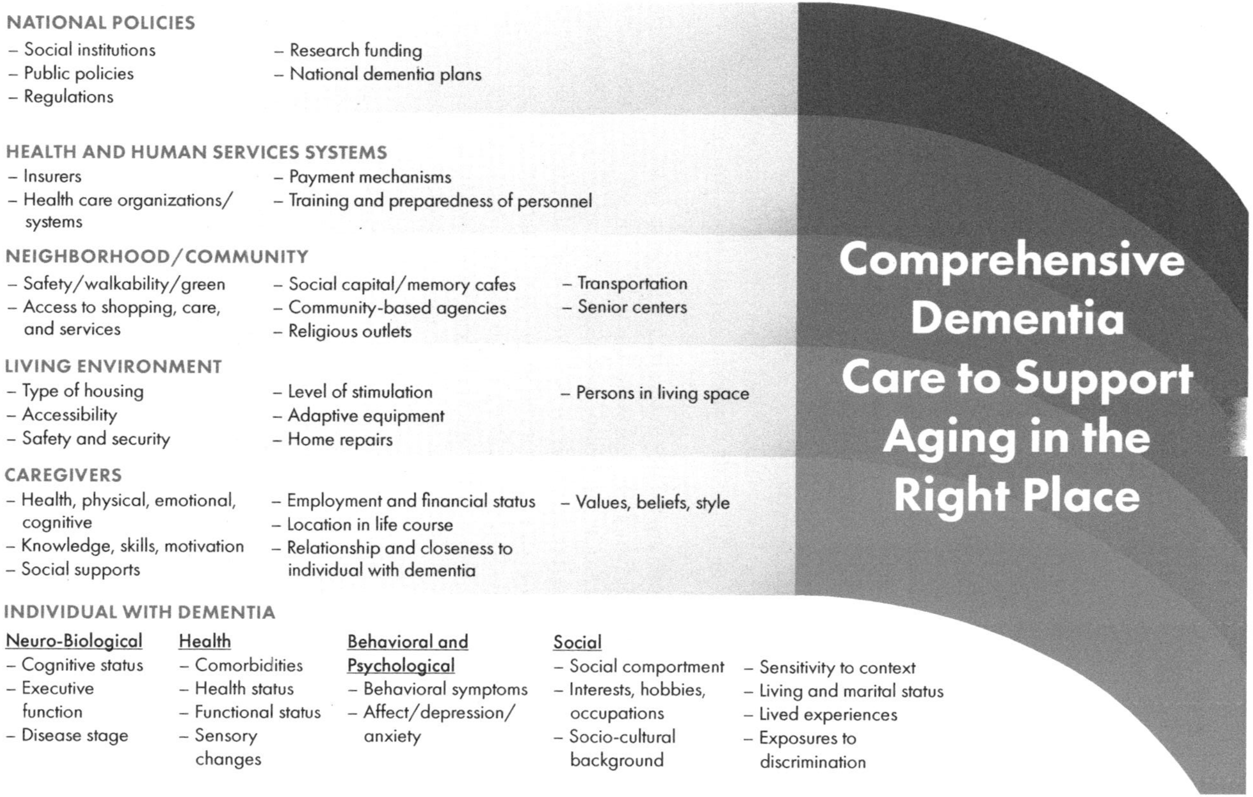

Comprehensive Dementia Care to Support Aging in the Right Place

NATIONAL POLICIES
– Social institutions
– Public policies
– Regulations
– Research funding
– National dementia plans

HEALTH AND HUMAN SERVICES SYSTEMS
– Insurers
– Health care organizations/systems
– Payment mechanisms
– Training and preparedness of personnel

NEIGHBORHOOD/COMMUNITY
– Safety/walkability/green
– Access to shopping, care, and services
– Social capital/memory cafes
– Community-based agencies
– Religious outlets
– Transportation
– Senior centers

LIVING ENVIRONMENT
– Type of housing
– Accessibility
– Safety and security
– Level of stimulation
– Adaptive equipment
– Home repairs
– Persons in living space

CAREGIVERS
– Health, physical, emotional, cognitive
– Knowledge, skills, motivation
– Social supports
– Employment and financial status
– Location in life course
– Relationship and closeness to individual with dementia
– Values, beliefs, style

INDIVIDUAL WITH DEMENTIA

Neuro-Biological
– Cognitive status
– Executive function
– Disease stage

Health
– Comorbidities
– Health status
– Functional status
– Sensory changes

Behavioral and Psychological
– Behavioral symptoms
– Affect/depression/anxiety

Social
– Social comportment
– Interests, hobbies, occupations
– Socio-cultural background
– Sensitivity to context
– Living and marital status
– Lived experiences
– Exposures to discrimination

FIGURE 4-1 A socio-ecological model to guide dementia care interventions.
SOURCE: Gitlin & Hodgson (2018, p. 1).

of programs targeting only the people living with dementia is inconsistent.

- Interventions are most successful when they are multicomponent—combining counseling, support, education, stress, mood, management, and skills training—and when they are tailored to the specific needs of either the individual living with dementia or the caregiver. Which groups benefit most from these interventions remains unclear because samples underrepresent racial, cultural, linguistic, ethnic, and geographic diversity.
- Most programs and their outcomes focus on mood, stress, health, quality of life, management of clinical symptoms, nursing home placement, and health utilization, but no single program is effective for all desired outcomes.
- The benefits of aging in place for the person's family unit are unclear. Relocation is typically due to a need for 24/7 supervision, mobility changes, and particular care and medical needs. Housing stock and housing repair needs are also unclear.
- Goals for aging at home should be balanced with family responsibilities and burdens, but the needs for people living alone are unclear.

Gitlin next described outcomes relevant to aging in place from the Tailored Activity Program, which supports individuals living with dementia, and the Creating Opportunities for Personal Empowerment (COPE) Program, which also supports the family caregivers (Clemson et al., 2021; Gitlin et al., 2010, 2021; Fortinsky et al., 2020; Pizzi et al., 2022). For example, caregivers who participated in the COPE Program were less upset and had higher confidence, and people living with dementia had fewer behavioral symptoms, reduced physical dependencies, and enhanced engagement. She asserted that improving well-being for caregivers is essential to enable aging in place for people living with dementia. Such interventions also increase home safety and save money for health systems. In the Tailored Activity Program, nearly 50% improvement was observed in health-related events that often trigger relocation for people living with dementia, and there was a reduction of more than 60% in the number of hospitalizations for program caregivers (Gitlin et al., 2021). In a COPE Program intervention that integrated an activity approach with caregiver support over a 4-month and a 9-month period, caregivers reported improved quality of life for the person with dementia, helping to keep that person living at home (Gitlin et al., 2010).

Gitlin shared additional data from a study on the use of the Adult Day Service Plus Program[1] over a 12-month period, which also showed an in-

---

[1] According to Alzheimers.gov, this program includes five components: care management, resource referrals, dementia education, situational counseling with emotional support and stress reduction techniques, and skills to manage behavioral symptoms (e.g., rejection of care, agitation, aggression).

crease in confidence and well-being among caregivers, as well as a decrease in depression (Gitlin et al., 2006, 2023; Reever et al., 2004). She explained that by increasing the ability of adult day service staff to provide evidence-based support for family caregivers, the families' ability to use adult day service increased and nursing home placement decreased by 50%. This study demonstrates that adult day services play a critical role in enabling aging in place for people with dementia. She pointed out that these outcomes were particularly important for Black caregivers in the study, who missed fewer of their own medical appointments by using the adult day service for those for whom they provide care.

Gitlin presented the results of another important study, which compared four interventions (Maximizing Independence at Home, New York University Caregiver, Alzheimer's and Dementia Care, and Adult Day Service Plus) to usual care. Results indicated that the interventions reduced nursing home admission, improved people's quality of life, increased cost savings for the community, increased time for people to spend in the community, provided more effective care, and reduced cost for delivery of care (Jutkowitz et al., 2023). She underscored that although these interventions share certain principles, they differ, which reinforces the notion that there will never be one single approach to meet all of the needs of both people living with dementia and their families.

In closing, Gitlin offered recommendations for four areas of research. First, new approaches to intervention development that involve interested parties (e.g., people living with dementia, caregivers, other family members, other stakeholders) and that use community participatory processes are needed. Mixed-methods research would help to understand feasibility, acceptability, effectiveness, and implementation outcomes of interventions for diverse individuals and communities. She underscored that researchers should consider context, delivery, sustainment, training, and cost from the start of intervention development, as well as considerations of equity at each methodological decision point. Additional research on the benefits of theory- and mechanism-based interventions would also be beneficial. She stressed that multilevel interventions, which add complexity but may reduce health disparities, should be prioritized. New interventions to support people with dementia who live alone, to offset responsibilities of family caregivers, to address a broader range of needs at different disease stages, to examine dyadic relationships, and to examine informal networks for decision making are also needed (Gitlin & Czaja, 2016).

Second, she said that new or adapted frameworks are needed to understand the meaning of and ability to age in the right place with dementia, such as expanded models to address the unique lived experience and the range of clinical symptoms of dementia that are triggers for relocation; expanded or adapted models to address the needs of family members and long-distance caregivers; models for people living alone; and theories and models to understand the impact of relocations for the individual and family members.

Third, she advocated for aligning outcome measures with stakeholder values; using targeted measurement strategies to reflect what matters most to families; and developing complex, multilevel metrics, including individual, family and caregiver, home environment, and community.

Finally, in terms of implementation, she suggested adopting new methodologies to move evidence more rapidly to practice so that more individuals and their families can benefit from interventions. She cautioned that many implementation challenges remain, including those related to payment models, regulatory issues, staffing availability, workflow alignment, and housing stock. As interventions move to the real world, evaluating implementation outcomes—such as acceptability, adoption, appropriateness, cost, feasibility, fidelity, penetration, and sustainability—will be critical (Proctor et al., 2011).

ADOPTING A HOUSING LENS

Jennifer Molinsky (Project Director of the Housing an Aging Society Program, Joint Center for Housing Studies, Harvard University) suggested that in addition to being viewed through medical and public health lenses, aging in place for people with dementia should be considered through a "housing lens"—that is, recognizing that where people live shapes challenges and limits solutions. Enabling aging in place for people with dementia requires understanding the complex interplay of housing as a home, as a site of care, as a financial burden, and as a physical environment. However, she explained, barriers to creating robust and effective interventions often arise because housing and health interventions emerge from different fields of research and are supported by different federal programs.

Although "aging in place" is interpreted differently by different people, Molinsky continued, definitions are rarely established in research or policy discussions. For example, for some people, aging in place means never leaving their homes; for others, it means staying in their homes only as long as possible. Additional definitions of aging in place include aging in a particular community, avoiding a nursing home, not moving between aged care facilities, or having choices about where to live. She pointed out that these differences have important implications for research, policy, and intervention (Forsyth & Molinsky, 2021; Molinsky & Forsyth, 2018; see Table 4-1). Furthermore, questions remain about individuals' *actual* preferences about where they would like to age, which are difficult to study and measure. She proposed adopting Gitlin's terminology of "aging in the

TABLE 4-1 Definitions of Aging in Place by Context

Definitions: Older people should/can:	Common rationales and/or motivations	Examples of policy implications	Examples of policy implications
Place-related			
1. Never move	Apparent simplicity of not moving, familiarity of environment, cost savings from not moving	Modify and service existing homes	Overhousing of older people, limiting supply; problems modifying housing; difficulties providing services; cost of in-home services at end of life; stuck in place
2. Stay put as long as possible	Simplicity, along with options late in life	Provide options for high care at end of life	If only the very ill are in purpose-built housing and nursing homes, then there could be concentrations of only the very sick in facilities; different understandings of as long as possible within household/family
3. Stay in the same vicinity	Allows downsizing/rightsizing but maintaining familiarity of area	Provide housing options nearby	Options may not be available or may be more costly
Services based			
4. Stay out of nursing homes	Can be anywhere, including with distant family	Flexible care options outside facilities; making nursing homes less repulsive	Inefficiency, lower quality care, household strain
5. Not move between aged care facilities	Not moving within care facility	Flexible care options in facilities	Regulatory barriers, staff training

(continued)

TABLE 4-1 Continued

Definitions: Older people should/can:	Common rationales and/or motivations	Examples of policy implications	Examples of policy implications
Control			
6. Have choices	Self-determination	Individual housing options	Moving may be a better option
7. Live out a multifaceted policy ideal	User choice, government cost savings	Provide housing options including upgrading; age-friendly communities	Moving may be a better option for fit

SOURCE: Forsyth & Molinsky (2021, Table 1). Reprinted with permission.

right place" or even "living in the right place," which highlights the benefits of aging instead of the degenerative process.

Molinsky noted that a housing lens provides insight because it centers on the complexities of where people live. Home is perceived as a platform for well-being based on its affordability, its physical suitability, its connections to supports and services, and its potential to contain memories and bolster one's sense of self. A housing lens also reveals housing disparities among older adults, such as unstable, inadequate, unaffordable, or inaccessible housing, as well as a lack of nearby caregivers or community supports. Finally, she indicated that a housing lens acknowledges that home-focused interventions depend on a home's stability, its resources, and its capacity to function as a site of care and a site of employment for both care providers and unpaid family members (Molinsky et al., 2022).

Applying this housing lens, Molinsky commented that older adults have unique housing challenges that affect their health. For example, although a lack of affordable housing affects everyone, it is more prevalent among older adults. Eleven million households in the United States use more than 30% of their income for housing, and more than five million households use more than 50% of their income for housing. She stressed that cost burdens are more prevalent among people of color; renters who have little control over their housing costs because of fixed resources (e.g., typical renters ages 65 and older have less than $6,000 in total net wealth); and owners with mortgages, which is the case for 27% of adults aged 80 and older (see Federal Reserve Board, 2019; U.S. Census Bureau, 2021). The gap between Black and White homeownership in particular is at a 30-year high among older adults, which affects the availability of resources to pay for care. These lifetime disadvantages compound in older age, widening disparities in health and financial security. People whose housing costs consume most of their resources have little to spend on other necessities, such as food, health care, transportation, and medication (U.S. Bureau of Labor Statistics, 2018). Yet, she noted, only one-third of older, low-income households who are eligible for housing assistance actually receive resources.

Furthermore, even though accessibility needs increase with age and an increasing number of older adults experience difficulties using and navigating their homes, Molinsky reported that less than 1% of all U.S. housing is fully wheelchair accessible, and only 3.5% offers basic accessibility features (U.S. Department of Housing and Urban Development, 2011, 2019). This lack of accessibility increases the risk for injury and increases the need to rely on others for assistance with activities of daily living. She added that caregivers are also an integral part of the residential setting to enable aging in place (Molinsky et al., 2023), yet they too may be experiencing stress related to increasing housing costs or decreasing housing quality.

Molinsky underscored that aging in place requires more than afford-able and accessible housing; many older adults need in-home support for household tasks and self-care, which is expensive and difficult to obtain. An increasing number of older adults are living in low-density areas, which may be difficult to reach for service providers. Loneliness is also a health risk, she noted, but many older people have a difficult time navigating spaces outside their homes and having access to transportation in their communities. Older people are also susceptible to weather-related risks, such as extreme heat or disruptions in health care after a storm. She noted that strategies to address some of these deficiencies in the current housing stock as well as to monitor and deliver better care in the home through technology, are being explored, but more research is needed into the disparities related to access to broadband, inaccessible housing, and housing insecurity that exclude people from these opportunities.

Molinsky also identified challenges in the coordination among housing, social services, and health care sectors needed to enable aging in place for people with dementia. For example, eligibility for subsidies differs across housing and service programs, leaving some people without critical supports. Furthermore, programs that make housing healthier and safer do not necessarily result in cost savings. Thus, additional research that investigates the health outcomes of housing or home-based interventions would be beneficial. Another significant challenge is a lack of data integration. For example, data on housing typically lack sufficient information on health, and health data typically lack sufficient details on housing. She cautioned against relying on data that focus on health care utilization, which could emphasize research questions based on cost savings rather than overall well-being or health (Molinsky et al., 2022).

Molinsky offered two concluding thoughts. First, using a housing lens to focus on older adults' homes in relation to their health and well-being (including financial security, social engagement, physical safety, and access to services and supports) serves as a reminder that older adults are more than their illnesses or clinical experiences. This perspective also helps illuminate the economics of aging in the United States, including the "dual burden" often posed by both housing and care costs. She asserted that considering where people live might change the way issues of aging in place are addressed.

Second, Molinsky said, increased dialogue between housing and health researchers could help illuminate the specific ways that housing influences health for people with dementia, support the development or integration of datasets that enable evaluation of housing-based interventions for health, highlight how disparities in housing affect the outcomes of other interventions, and support outcome measures beyond those focused on health care utilization (Molinsky et al., 2022).

EVALUATION: TOWARD A VALUE PROPOSITION

Louise Lafortune (Principal Research Associate, Cambridge Public Health, Cambridge University) observed that "home" is embedded in interconnected community, social, and policy environments, and the aging experience can be successful only to the extent that these environments enable such an outcome. She argued that programs that support aging in place both for people with and without dementia should optimize the fit between individuals and their living environments. However, she pointed out that the evidence base on what works, for whom, and under what circumstances is limited, creating barriers to implement and scale interventions.

Lafortune asserted that a successful later life is possible at all stages of health and frailty if supports are well targeted and delivered equitably: that is, by understanding the factors that influence successful aging, developing interventions and solutions that are tailored to people's needs, and demonstrating what works and adds value. Although evaluation efforts of interventions at the individual level are increasing and evidence is accumulating, the evidence for interventions that target dyads, social networks, cities, and policies is lacking.

Using the framework from the World Health Organization for age-friendly cities and communities, Lafortune discussed how capacity is being built for such evaluations. Age-friendly cities and communities leverage an approach in which policies, services, settings, and structures support and enable people to age actively (World Health Organization, n.d.). These communities "are created by removing physical and social barriers and implementing policies, systems, services, products and technologies that address the social determinants of healthy aging, and enable people, even when they lose capacity, to continue to do the things they value" (United Nations Decade of Healthy Ageing, n.d., p. 13). Much has been invested in these communities, but further research is needed to better understand how and if they are effective.

Lafortune emphasized that because there will never be enough funding to evaluate all that needs to be evaluated, her team is building capacity for evaluation by providing the practice-focused tools and the understanding of the process for evaluating complex interventions. The first step in building this capacity was creating a survey to understand the needs of members of the U.K. network of age-friendly communities, which highlighted a lack of capacity for evaluation in practice. However, to sustain investment in age-friendly initiatives, demonstrating their impact is critical. Thus, her team developed a process evaluation tool in collaboration with practice stakeholders that identifies and assesses the "active ingredients" of a sustainable age-friendly community. The tool included ten evidence input areas to guide information collection: political support; leadership and governance; financial and human resources; involvement of older people; priorities based on needs assessment; application of existing frameworks for assessing age-friendliness; provision; interventions rooted in evidence base; coordination, collaboration, and interlinkages; and monitoring and evaluation (Buckner et al., 2018; Buckner, Pope et al., 2019). She explained that this evaluation tool for age-friendly communities was piloted for an intervention in Liverpool, in a dementia-friendly community in Sheffield, and to inform the creation of a new community in Northstowe. The tool used a scale of 1–5 to determine whether enough evidence exists in each area to assess both the process and the progress of the age-friendly communities. In one instance, the tool revealed that despite political support, leadership and governance were lacking, which made it difficult to monitor progress and implement the right types of interventions.

After this pilot experience, Lafortune and her team became involved in a national evaluation of dementia-friendly communities in England called the DEMCOM study.[2] Providing context on this effort, she noted that in 2015, the Prime Minister's Challenge set a target to have more than half of England's population living in areas recognized as dementia-friendly communities by 2020. She noted that these communities, guided and officially recognized by the Alzheimer's Society, vary by size and shape, but the common goal is to ensure that people affected by dementia can continue to be active and to be valued citizens. The DEMCOM study attempted to better understand the characteristics and areas of focus of dementia-friendly communities, how different types of communities enable people affected by dementia to live well, what is needed to sustain the communities, what value the communities generate, and how the communities can be assessed.

Lafortune and the DEMCON team piloted the evaluation tool developed for age-friendly communities in two dementia-friendly communities, conducted a survey among national stakeholders, and developed a revised evaluation framework better suited to evaluate dementia-friendly communities and to guide evaluators' work. The revised framework included thematic domains—activities and environments, basis of dementia-friendly community, leadership and governance, resources, and monitoring and evaluation—and crosscutting issues—evolution, equalities, and involvement of people affected by dementia (Buckner et al., 2022; Buckner, Darlington et al., 2019; Darlington et al., 2020; Mathie et al., 2022; Woodward et al., 2019). A suite of evaluation resources for dementia-friendly communities that accompanies the framework includes a theory of change tool (i.e., how dementia-friendly communities can make a difference and what outcomes

---

[2] https://arc-eoe.nihr.ac.uk/research-implementation/research-themes/ageing-and-multi-morbidity/demcom-study-national-evaluation

they can achieve at what stage) and a matrix for assessing community maturity (which can inform community aspirations; Buckner et al., 2022).

Lafortune also provided an economic perspective on dementia-friendly communities, describing efforts from the DEMCOM study to implement simple tools to better understand the resources that drive these communities. Increased awareness of these resources makes it possible to inform decision making for investments and sustain key activities in dementia-friendly communities. Using an approach known as social return on investment (i.e., an approach building on cost-benefit analysis) and data derived from DEMCOM to explore the social value of dementia-friendly communities for people with dementia, she and her team found that dementia-friendly communities have the potential to generate a significant social return on investment.

For age-friendly community initiatives in particular, however, Lafortune noted that little is known about short- and long-term benefits and resource implications. She described current efforts to understand the health-related outcomes of age-friendly community interventions and their social value for older adults, as well as the resources needed to sustain these complex interventions at different geographical scales. Preliminary evidence from a systematic review suggests that aging-well interventions, including those targeting people with dementia, generate a positive social return on investment.[3] The next step is to explore how that information can be used in practice to support implementation.

In closing, Lafortune offered suggestions for future work. She encouraged the formation of interdisciplinary research programs to create the knowledge to understand the mechanism of action of complex interventions, their impact on phenotypes of aging in context, and barriers to the implementation of research findings. She also proposed that evaluations embrace the complexity of aging in place for people with dementia by engaging older adults and practice stakeholders from the design to the implementation of evaluation, developing a theory of change to guide impact assessment, and tailoring research questions and methods to the maturity of the intervention. She noted that economic and social value implications need to be better understood to help implement and sustain aging in place initiatives. Lastly, she encouraged researchers to embrace an equity lens to avoid intervention-generated inequalities.[4]

---

[3] An overview of the review can be found at: https://arc-eoe.nihr.ac.uk/research-implementation/research-themes/population-evidence-and-data-science/evidencing-social

[4] https://forequity.uk/hiat

DISCUSSION

Sharing questions from workshop participants, Jennifer Ailshire (Associate Professor of Gerontology and Sociology, Assistant Dean of Research, and Associate Dean of International Programs and Global Initiatives, University of Southern California; planning committee member) moderated a discussion among the session's three speakers. She highlighted the speakers' points about the costs and benefits of interventions, strategies to reduce future costs, and renewed concepts of aging in place that are determined by the least financial hardship. She invited the speakers to share any additional commentary on issues of cost and aging in place.

Lafortune emphasized the importance of understanding both the costs related to people's living conditions and the costs of interventions. She explained that the effects of an aging in place intervention on the utilization of health care services can be measured relatively easily as long as people recognize that this is an outcome to support the sustainability of the intervention. An intervention can be deemed "cost-effective" when additional health benefits accrue from investing in that particular intervention. However, she pointed out, the budget implications of rolling out an intervention are often not captured in these analyses. Thus, unless an evaluation program captures the effects of the intervention on health outcomes, as well as the consequence of maintaining people in that state of health, funders may not understand why they should invest in an intervention.

Gitlin noted that defining cost is important, especially because decreasing societal financial cost could increase family caregiver financial cost. Furthermore, because U.S. systems are fragmented, even when community-based programs help people to remain living at home and reduce health care utilization, they do not share in the cost savings that benefit the health care systems. Evaluating complex financial elements is critical, she continued, owing to different implications for different people.

Emily Agree (Research Professor and Associate Director, Hopkins Population Center, Johns Hopkins University; planning committee chair) wondered whether any financial and housing problems could be addressed if Medicaid paid for assisted living. In response, Molinsky underscored that assisted living is not accessible for most people in the United States because they cannot afford to pay for it out of pocket and do not qualify for a subsidy. She urged researchers to explore how to better support low-income people, as well as how supporting housing and care together could improve this situation. Gitlin agreed that finances are a significant issue for families, especially when thinking about living situations, and they would benefit from increased guidance about and awareness of alternative options for care.

Ailshire pointed out that sometimes institutionalized care may be the best outcome for people with dementia and their caregivers. She asked about studies that compare quality of life outcomes and life expectancy for those aging in a nursing home versus those aging at home. Lafortune replied that comparing quality of life in these two different settings is difficult: people in nursing homes tend to be more advanced in the disease than people living at home, which complicates the potential for a direct comparison. Molinsky agreed and noted that comparisons about quality of life often include a self-selection problem. Although quality of life is an important issue, she continued, much of the current evidence is only anecdotal; data to evaluate the true value of different settings in which people age are needed.

Gitlin raised the issue that extreme variability in care exists across facilities, and no known databases help address this problem. Elena Fazio (Director of the Office of Alzheimer's Disease and Alzheimer's Disease-Related Dementias Strategic Coordination, Division of Behavioral and Social Research, National Institute on Aging [NIA]) mentioned that the National Health and Aging Trends Study follows individuals from setting to setting, providing a robust data resource for researchers in the United States interested in studying quality of life across settings. However, she said that more data that follow people across settings are needed, especially given the complexity of meaningfully defining and measuring quality of life.

Reflecting on Ailshire's and others' comments that aging at home may not be optimal for several reasons, Lis Nielsen (NIA) posed a question about whether deferring transition to facility-based care should still be a primary goal or if researchers should also consider an agenda around how people can age well in place in appropriate facility-based environments. Molinsky championed the value of considering multiple settings in discussions on aging in place and indicated that robust data are needed to evaluate components of both health and home, such as cost, accessibility, and interconnectedness with other community services.

Nielsen then asked how to better prepare employees at community sites, volunteers, and professional care staff to support people living with dementia to age in place. Lafortune said that in the United Kingdom, the Alzheimer's Society developed the Dementia Friends Program,[5] which trains people in different communities using a "train the trainers" approach. For example, in one of her dementia-friendly community case studies, one grocery store employee was trained to train his employees to recognize signs of dementia in shoppers. Regina Shih (Professor of Epidemiology and Health Policy and Management, Emory University, and Adjunct Policy researcher, RAND)

---

[5]The program is an initiative of the Alzheimer's Society; https://www.alzheimers.org.uk/get-involved/dementia-friendly-communities/dementia-friends

noted that a few villages in the Village to Village Network are beginning to train their staff using the AARP Dementia-Friendly Communities Program.[6] Gitlin described online training programs that are available for community-based health care providers and aides, although these options have not been rigorously tested in terms of what works best for each group in terms of improving care delivery and outcomes. She added that the information that should be transmitted about good dementia care is well known, but gaps remain in how to disseminate this information to individuals and to monitor outcomes.[7]

REFERENCES

Buckner, S., Darlington, N., Woodward, M., Buswell, M., Mathie, E., Arthur, A., Lafortune, L., Killett, A., Mayrhofer, A., Thurman, J., & Goodman, C. D. (2019). Dementia friendly communities in England: A scoping study. *International Journal of Geriatric Psychiatry*, 16. https://doi.org/10.1002/gps.5123

Buckner, S., Lafortune, L., Darlington, N., Dickinson, A., Killett, A., Mathie, E., Mayrhofer, A., Woodward, M., & Goodman, C. (2022). A suite of evaluation resources for dementia friendly communities: Development and guidance for use. *Dementia: The International Journal of Social Research and Practice*, 21(8), 2381–2401.

Buckner, S., Mattocks, C., Rimmer, M., & Lafortune, L. (2018). An evaluation tool for age-friendly and dementia friendly communities. *Working with Older People*, 22(1), 48–58. https://doi.org/10.1108/WWOP-11-2017-0032

Buckner, S., Pope, D., Mattocks, C., Lafortune, L., Dherani, M., & Bruce, N. (2019). Developing age-friendly cities: An evidence-based evaluation tool. *Journal of Population Ageing*, 12, 203–223. https://link.springer.com/article/10.1007/s12062-017-9206-2

Clemson, L., Laver, K., Rahja, M., Culph, J., Scanlan, J. N., Day, S., Comans, T., Jeon, Y.-H., Low, L.-F., Crotty, M., Kurrle, S., Cations, M., Piersol, C. V., & Gitlin, L. N. (2021). Implementing a reablement intervention, "Care of people with dementia in their environments (COPE)": A hybrid implementation-effectiveness study. *The Gerontologist*, 61(6), 965–976.

Darlington, N., Arthur, A., Woodward, M., Buckner, S., Killet, A., Lafortune, L., Mathie, E., Mayrhofer, A., Thurman J., & Goodman, C. (2020). A survey of the experience of living with dementia in a dementia-friendly community. *Dementia*, 20(5). https://journals.sagepub.com/doi/10.1177/1471301220965552

Federal Reserve Board. (2019). 2019 Survey of Consumer Finances. https://www.federalreserve.gov/econres/scf_2019.htm

Forsyth, A., & Molinsky, J. (2021). What is aging in place? Confusions and contradictions. *Housing Policy Debate*, 31(2), 181–196. https://doi.org/10.1080/10511482.2020.1793795

Fortinsky, R. H., Gitlin, L. N., Pizzi, L. T., Piersol, C. V., Grady, J., Robison, J. T., Molony, S., & Wakefield, D. (2020). Effectiveness of the care of persons with dementia in their environments intervention when embedded in a publicly funded home- and community-based service program. *Innovation in Aging*, 4(6).

Gitlin, L. N., & Czaja, S. J. (2016). *Behavioral intervention research: Designing, evaluating, and implementing*. Springer Publishing Company.

---

[6] https://www.aarp.org/livable-communities/network-age-friendly-communities/
[7] See the end of Chapter 5 for a summary of this session and the following one.

Gitlin, L. N., & Hodgson, N. (2018). *Better living with dementia: Implications for individuals, families, communities, and societies.* Academic Press.

Gitlin, L. N., Reever, K., Dennis, M. P., Mathieu, E., & Hauck, W. (2006). Enhancing quality of life of families who use adult day services: Short- and long-term effects of the Adult Day Services Plus Program. *The Gerontologist, 46,* 630–639.

Gitlin, L. N., Roth, D. L., Marx, K., Parker, L. J., Koeuth, S., Dabelko-Schoeny, H., Anderson, K., & Gaugler, J. E. (2023). Embedding caregiver support within adult day services: Outcomes of a multi-site trial. *The Gerontologist.* https://doi.org/10.1093/geront/gnad107

Gitlin, L. N., Winter, L., Dennis, M. P., Hodgson, N., & Hauck, W. W. (2010). A biobehavioral home-based intervention and the well-being of patients with dementia and their caregivers: The COPE randomized trial. *Journal of the American Medical Association, 304*(9), 983–991.

Gitlin, L. N., Marx, K., Piersol, C. V., Hodgson, N. A., Huang, J., Roth, D. L. & Lykestsos, C. (2021). Effects of the Tailored Activity Program (TAP) on dementia-related symptoms, health events and caregiver wellbeing: A randomized controlled trial. *BMC Geriatrics (21)*581. https://doi.org/10.1186/s12877-021-02511-4

Jutkowitz, E., Pizzi, L. T., Shewmaker, P., Alarid-Escudero, F., Epstein-Lubow, G., Prioli, K. M., Gaugler, J. E., & Gitlin, L. N. (2023). Cost effectiveness of non-drug interventions that reduce nursing home admissions for people living with dementia. *Alzheimer's & Dementia, 19*(9), 3867–3893.

Mathie, E., Arthur, A., Killet, A., Darlington, N., Buckner, S., Lafortune, L., Mayrhofer, A., Dickinson, E., Woodward, M., & Goodman, C. (2022). Dementia friendly communities: The involvement of people living with dementia. *Dementia: The International Journal of Social Research and Practice, 21*(4). https://doi.org/10.1177/14713012211073200

Molinsky, J., & Forsyth, A. (2018). Housing, the built environment, and the good life. *The Hastings Report, 48*(S3). https://doi.org/10.1002/hast.914

Molinsky, J., Berlinger, N., & Hu, B. (2022). *Advancing housing and health equity for older adults: Pandemic innovations and policy ideas.* Joint Center for Housing Studies. https://www.jchs.harvard.edu/sites/default/files/reports/files/Harvard_JCHS_Hastings_Advancing_Housing_Health_Equity_for_Older_Adults_2022.pdf

Molinsky, J., Scheckler, S., & Hu, B. (2023). *Centering the home in conversations about digital technology to support older adults aging in place.* Joint Center for Housing Studies.

Pizzi, L. T., Jutkowitz, E., Prioli, K. M., Lu, E., Babcock, Z., McAbee-Sevick, H., Wakefield, D. B., Robison, J., Molony, S., Piersol, C. V., Gitlin, L. N., & Fortinsky, R. H. (2022). Cost–benefit analysis of the COPE program for persons living with dementia: Toward a payment model. *Innovation in Aging, 6*(1).

Proctor, E., Silmere, H., Raghavan, R., Hovmand, P., Aarons, G., Bunger, A., Griffey, R., & Hensley, M. (2011). Outcomes for implementation research: Conceptual distinctions, measurement challenges, and research agenda. *Administration and Policy in Mental Health, 38*(2), 65–76.

Reever, K. E., Mathieu, E., Dennis, M. P., & Gitlin, L. N. (2004). Adult Day Services Plus: Augmenting adult day centers with systematic care management for family caregivers. *Alzheimer's Care Quarterly, 5*(4), 332–339.

United Nations Decade of Healthy Ageing. (n.d.). *WHO's work on the UN Decade of Health Ageing (2021–2030).* https://www.who.int/initiatives/decade-of-healthy-ageing

U.S. Bureau of Labor Statistics. (2018). *Consumer Expenditures in 2018.* https://www.bls.gov/opub/reports/consumer-expenditures/2018/pdf/home.pdf

U.S. Census Bureau. (2021). *2021 American Community Survey.* https://www.census.gov/programs-surveys/acs/news/data-releases.2021.html

U.S. Department of Housing and Urban Development. (2011). *American Housing Survey for the United States: 2011.* https://www.census.gov/library/publications/2013/demo/h150-11.html

___. (2019). *American Housing Survey.* https://www.census.gov/programs-surveys/ahs/data.2019.List_1739896299.html#list-tab-List_1739896299

Woodward, M., Arthur, A., Darlington, N., Buckner, S., Killett, A., Thurman, J., Buswell, M., Lafortune, L., Mathie, E., Mayrhofer, A., & Goodman, C. (2019). The place of dementia friendly communities in England and its relationship with epidemiological need. *International Journal of Geriatrics, 34,* 67–71. https://doi.org/10.1002/gps.4987

World Health Organization. (n.d.). The WHO Age-friendly Cities Framework. *Age-Friendly World.* https://extranet.who.int/agefriendlyworld/age-friendly-cities-framework

5

Social Services and Other Supports

Key Points Highlighted by Presenters

- Community paramedics could help support aging in place by leveraging their universal presence and extensive medical skills, as well as by preventing and substituting for emergency department visits; however, community paramedicine infrastructure and programs would benefit from further development and testing. (**SHAH**)

- As dementia progresses, paid caregiving often replaces some of the unpaid care previously provided by family members during an earlier stage of dementia; however, even when receiving paid care, older adults with dementia are more likely than those without dementia to experience adverse consequences owing to unmet needs. (**FABIUS**)

- Several different systems play a role in delivering care to people with dementia and providing support to their families; cross-sector collaboration is critical as the field of dementia care continues to evolve. (**TREJO**)

The fourth session of the workshop focused on the integration of social services and other support environments, which is a critical aspect of multilevel approaches and socio-ecological models to enable dementia care and research. Speakers and workshop participants had been asked to address the following questions: How can local health and social service systems be incorporated into community-level efforts to support people living with dementia, help them to stay in their own homes longer, and minimize adverse consequences? What is the role of physicians and other health care providers to improve quality of life and reduce hospitalization and institutionalization?

EMERGENCY COMMUNITY RESOURCES

Manish Shah (Professor and Chair of the BerbeeWalsh Department of Emergency Medicine, University of Wisconsin–Madison) underscored that people living with dementia have complex, often unpredictable medical and social needs. They often rely on a hospital emergency department (ED) for acute illness care because of limited access to outpatient care, delays in seeking care, and limited availability of rapid outpatient diagnostic testing and therapeutic interventions (Beck et al., 2020; Feng et al., 2014; LaMantia et al., 2016). However, he noted that EDs—with their bright lights, noise, constant interruptions, and overall busy environments—are not an optimal solution to meet the acute care needs of people living with dementia. ED care primarily focuses on identifying and treating life-threatening and time-sensitive conditions, and ED providers have limited health information about people with dementia who visit an ED for an acute issue, creating discontinuity in care (Hwang et al., 2022).

For acute care among people living with dementia who are aging in place with their care partners, Shah proposed two approaches to eliminate or reduce ED visits: (1) identify developing conditions early through assessment and monitoring, educating people living with dementia and their care partners about dementia progression and acute illnesses, and increasing communication channels between a patient and their caregiver dyad and the primary health care team, as well as social services and other community supports; and (2) assess people living with dementia at home and deliver advanced acute illness care in person or via telemedicine, educating and coaching people living with dementia and their care partners about how to handle a particular acute illness and when to seek further care, and collaborating with medical and social services to ensure proper follow-up and support for acute illnesses (Jacobsohn et al., 2019).

Shah then turned to the emergency medical services (EMS) system. Traditionally, it has focused on providing urgent prehospital treatment and stabilization for serious illnesses and injuries, as well as transporting patients to hospitals for care (Shah, 2006). However, the more modern EMS model embraces a public health role; serves as the community safety net (not just for acute illnesses); leverages its universal presence to help anyone, anywhere; and responds rapidly. For example, the "community paramedic," a new type of EMS provider, functions outside of the usual emergency response and transport role to reduce ED and hospital use and to support the community's health. A community paramedic performs public health and prevention activities such as vaccination and screening, educates and coaches patients and care partners, assesses and monitors patients, delivers advanced care to patients without transporting them to the hospital, and collaborates with community-wide resources to support patients. Shah highlighted the strengths and limitations of this approach. On the positive side, a community paramedic is universally present, is highly respected, is knowledgeable about acute illnesses, and has advanced diagnostic and therapeutic capabilities. However, community paramedics have limited disease-specific knowledge, limited mobile diagnostic technologies, and limited ability to access information from and collaborate across systems of care. Furthermore, the scope of practice and licensing are currently unclear, and no dedicated funding is available for the community paramedicine approach.

Shah noted that despite these challenges, emerging evidence suggests that community paramedics could be a valuable resource to help people with dementia to age in place. In terms of efforts to prevent ED visits, he remarked that his team has been adapting the Resources Enhancing Alzheimer's Caregiver Health (REACH) model[1] to the emergency care setting. The REACH model has been employed by community paramedics in collaboration with primary care clinics to support a pilot effort, funded by the National Institute on Aging (NIA), among people who live in a rural community. This pilot addressed communication and electronic health record challenges and barriers; demonstrated good engagement and participation by community paramedics, people living with dementia, caregivers, and community clinics; and resulted in promising qualitative evidence.

Shah described another effort to prevent ED visits by improving care transitions. He noted that after discharge from an ED, people living with dementia have extremely high rates of return visits to the ED within 30 days. He and his team adapted the care transitions intervention[2] to create the community paramedic transitions intervention, which is delivered to older patients being discharged from the ED to their homes. He indicated that ED patients with cognitive impairment who received the intervention had significantly reduced odds of a return visit to the ED within 30 days (Shah et al., 2022).

In terms of efforts to substitute for ED visits, Shah described a recent study that tested a high-intensity telemedicine program. It provided home-

---

[1] https://www.icpsr.umich.edu/web/ICPSR/studies/03678
[2] https://caretransitions.health

based acute illness care for older adults living both independently and in assisted living, delivered by technicians with telemedicine and laboratory testing capabilities. The technicians went to the person's residence, facilitated the telemedicine visit, obtained laboratory specimens, and took the person to the hospital for further testing if needed. He said that for a subgroup of participants with dementia, the intervention decreased ED use by 24% (Gillespie et al., 2019).

Turning to a discussion of methodological considerations for these approaches, Shah indicated that these studies require evaluation for diverse groups of people living with dementia and their care partners (e.g., those with limited English proficiency, those living in rural or low-resource communities), implementation science approaches for translation to practice that involve community members and community organizations, and randomized and pragmatic clinical trials that include diverse populations to evaluate the effectiveness of interventions and inform necessary modifications. Furthermore, he said, infrastructure research and development for community paramedics is needed to support the needs and care of both people with dementia and their care partners.

Developing and testing necessary communication linkages and efficiencies is particularly critical—for example, the interoperability of medical and social service providers, accessibility of integrated medical and social service records, parsing of records for use, and applicability of artificial intelligence. Another opportunity is to develop and test devices to monitor and diagnose acutely ill people with dementia who live at home (e.g., telemonitoring and telehealth technologies, as well as viral and bacterial panels). He noted that artificial intelligence could also be used in collaboration with some of these technologies to reduce the oversight time of providers. Programmatic research and development is also essential, he continued. For instance, to prevent ED visits, he suggested developing and testing a community paramedic–led approach to address the educational and social support needs of people living with dementia and their care partners during acute illness and as the dementia evolves, and to develop and test community paramedic–led programs to enhance transitions between any sites. To substitute for ED visits, he advocated for developing and testing community paramedic–led approaches to deliver acute illness care to people living with dementia without transporting them to the hospital. Although initial research is promising, he stressed that much work remains to improve care options for people aging in place with dementia.

PAID CARE AND FAMILY CAREGIVERS

Chanee Fabius (Assistant Professor in the Department of Health Policy and Management, Bloomberg School of Public Health, John Hopkins University) provided an overview of paid care, which provides assistance with routine daily activities (e.g., bathing, dressing, preparing meals, administering medication) for people with disabilities. Paid care is found in both traditional home- and community-based settings and in residential care settings, such as assisted living. The goal of delivering paid care typically is to delay or replace the need for nursing home services. Paid care is supported by waivers through Medicaid's home- and community-based services (HCBS) and administered by states, private pay, or Medicare Home Health. As a result of Medicaid HCBS rebalancing efforts over the past several decades, she explained, many state priorities for financing have shifted from institutional care to HCBS; this creates significant variability in how people access services and what services they can receive, which makes it difficult to assess care quality.

Fabius indicated that paid care is delivered in the United States by the direct care workforce, which is comprised of home care workers (approximately 2.6 million personal care aides, home health aides, and nursing assistants who support individuals in private homes), residential care aides (647,500 personal care aides, home health aides, and nursing assistants who assist individuals in group homes, assisted living communities, and other residential care settings), and nursing assistants (471,000 workers who provide services to individuals living in skilled nursing homes). Home care workers are primarily female immigrants of racial and ethnic minority groups. The national median hourly wage for home care workers was $12.98/hour in 2020 (PHI, 2022).

Presenting an overview of data from the 2011 National Health and Aging Trends Study on the percentage of older adults receiving paid and unpaid care, Fabius noted that 50% of people with three or more self-care or mobility needs receive paid assistance. More than 44% of people in the same category receive both paid and unpaid care (i.e., from family or other caregivers) to address their needs (Freedman & Spillman, 2014). She added that paid and unpaid caregivers often collaborate to provide care to older adults with disabilities who live in their communities.

Fabius turned to a discussion of the racial and ethnic disparities in paid care, for which research on access and experiences is limited and mixed. Some evidence reveals disparities in outcomes such as hospitalizations: For example, among HCBS participants, Black older adults with dementia are more likely to experience hospitalization. However, observed differences in access may be the result of several factors, such as service availability in a particular area or a lack of culturally tailored services (e.g., lack of non-English-speaking agency staff). In Medicare Home Health in particular, racial and ethnic disparities have been observed in the initiation, provision, and quality of services (see Fashaw-Walters et al., 2022; Gorges et al., 2019; Joynt Maddox et al., 2018; Shippee et al., 2022; Yeboah-Korang et al., 2011).

Fabius indicated that older adults living with dementia are more likely to use paid care than those without dementia. Dementia-specific targeted supports are available in some states (e.g., through Medicaid HCBS and assisted living), and limited dementia-specific training is available for direct care workers. However, as a result of disparities in dementia prevalence and level of disability, people who are racial and ethnic minorities that receive paid care may have different service needs than their White counterparts (see Cornell et al., 2020; Fabius et al., 2020, 2022; Garfield et al., 2015; Kasper et al., 2015).

Fabius noted that the use of paid care also varies by stage of dementia. Reckrey et al. (2020) used the 2015 National Health and Aging Trends Study to characterize paid caregiving frequency among community-dwelling older adults with dementia and to identify factors associated with receiving paid care. They found that weekly paid caregiving hours for those with advanced dementia replaced some of the unpaid care previously provided by family caregivers during an earlier stage of dementia. However, even when receiving paid care, these older adults with dementia were more likely than those without dementia to experience adverse consequences from unmet needs (Fabius et al., 2022). In another study that leveraged Maryland Medicaid HCBS data for a sample of older adults, significant differences in low social engagement, hospitalizations, and emergency room use were not observed between those with dementia and those without dementia over a 90-day period; however, a significant number of participants reported not participating in activities they enjoyed. Fabius said that these data suggest that social engagement is a key component of quality of life that should be examined further (Fabius, Millar, et al., 2023).

Fabius also discussed the relationship between family caregivers and paid care. Family caregivers of older adults who receive paid care often report spending time managing paid caregivers in the home, including monitoring and training the caregivers and coordinating care (Reckrey et al., 2022). Family caregivers of people with dementia are typically more involved in service coordination than those of people without dementia. Fabius indicated that among family caregivers, racial differences exist for caregiving intensity, level of disability of the care recipient, available financial resources, and caregiving experiences. She remarked that people from racial and ethnic minorities are more often caring for older adults with dementia with a greater level of disability and with fewer financial resources than nonminorities; however, these caregivers less often report emotional strain or burden related to caregiving (see Fabius et al., 2020; Parker & Fabius, 2022; Reckrey et al., 2022; Travers et al., 2023).

Fabius indicated that family caregivers of older participants in Maryland Medicaid HCBS experienced less burden than the general caregiving population (Fabius, Millar, et al., 2023), but family caregivers of older adults with dementia were more likely to feel overwhelmed, distressed, angry, depressed, or unable to continue caregiving than those caring for older adults without dementia (Fabius, Millar, et al., 2023). Among caregivers of people with dementia, experiences varied when paid care was used. Those receiving full-time paid care reported the most significant benefit (e.g., less exhaustion; Reckrey et al., 2021): Fabius noted, however, that full-time paid care is out of reach financially for many people.

Given this evidence about existing racial and ethnic disparities in paid care use and experiences and the need to improve paid care for older adults with dementia and their caregivers (with consideration for their cultural experiences and for the roles of and implications for the direct care workforce), Fabius stressed that innovative approaches are needed. She shared the following strategies related to paid care that have been implemented or could be implemented in the future to support all older adults with dementia as well as their family caregivers. First, after conducting qualitative interviews in Maryland, Fabius, Wec et al. (2023) found that communication and collaboration about aspects of care between family caregivers and clinical care teams is critically important for people living with dementia.

Second, Fabius and her team developed a long-term services and support environment framework to help researchers and policymakers better understand state and local place-based characteristics associated with care quality and access experiences of older adults across three domains—social and economic, health care and social services delivery, and built and natural physical environment—and three levels—societal, community, and household (Fabius, Okoye, et al., 2023): see Table 5-1.

Fabius commented that efforts to better support older adults with dementia and their caregivers are also under way at the national level. The 2023 National Research Summit on Care, Services, and Supports for Persons Living with Dementia and Their Care Partners/Caregivers had three recommendations:[3]

(1) Examine how health care policies and payment models differentially affect access and quality of care received by people living with dementia in community settings to guide interventions;
(2) Conduct culturally informed research on caregivers' well-being and the provision of caregiving supports and services; and
(3) Conduct research to strengthen the direct care workforce, including increasing available data, understanding the interactions within caregiving teams, and developing equitable interventions.

---

[3] https://www.nia.nih.gov/2023-dementia-care-summit

TABLE 5-1 A Long-Term Services and Support Environment Framework

Environmental Domains	Environmental Levels		
	Societal (state or federal)	Community Context (local, neighborhood)	Household
	Quality (e.g., quality of services, adequacy of policy implementation)		
Social and economic			
Economic status	SNAP generosity	SDI; poverty, education	Income and assets; education; receipt of public assistance
Sociocultural factors	Community participation	Crime; social cohesion; segregation	Religiosity; language; cultural beliefs
Health care and social services delivery			
Health care/LTSS financing	Medicaid HCBS generosity; minimum wage; MLTSS presence; Medicare Advantage enrollees; Tritle III/OAA spending	Medicaid enrollment; health insurance mix; Medicare spending	Medicaid-enrolled; source of paid help (e.g., state Medicaid program; private pay; long-term care insurance
Direct care workforce	Training requirements	Supply, wages	Presence and type of paid help
Family caregiving	Availability of state paid family leave, paid sick leave	Number of older/disabled person services (e.g., adult day care services)	Relationship of caregiver, hours of care Food stamps, meal delivery

Built and natural physical environment

Transportation/land use	Presence of state coordination council	Zoning, population density	Car ownership, driving status, transportation
Communication infrastructure	State web accessibility regulations	Proportion of population with broadband internet	Internet use
Housing infrastructure		Household value-to-income ratio, median housing stock age	Housing quality, residence type, rent *vs.* own

NOTES: HCBS, home- and community-based services; LTSS, long-term services and supports; MLTSS, managed long-term services and supports; OAA, Older Americans Act; SDI, Social Deprivation Index; SNAP, Supplemental Nutrition Assistance Program.
SOURCE: Fabius, Okoye, et al. (2023).

The 2022 National Strategy to Support Family Caregivers offered five goals:[4]

(1) Increase awareness of and outreach to family caregivers;
(2) Advance partnerships and engagement with family caregivers;
(3) Strengthen services and supports for family caregivers;
(4) Ensure financial and workplace security for family caregivers; and
(5) Expand data, research, and evidence-based practices to support family caregivers.

In addition, Fabius reported, the 2023 White House Executive Order on Increasing Access to High-Quality Care and Supporting Caregivers[5] serves to improve the affordability of long-term services and support, improve access to home-based care for veterans, enhance job quality and compensation for the direct care workforce, and support family caregivers. In closing, Fabius underscored that policy, research, and practice all play a key role in increasing knowledge and addressing issues related to paid care delivery disparities and family caregivers.

LOS ANGELES COUNTY AGING AND DISABILITIES DEPARTMENT

Laura Trejo (Director, Los Angeles County Aging and Disabilities Department) described her work to change policy at the macro and micro levels to ensure that the needs of Los Angeles County's aging population and people with disabilities are met, as well as to demonstrate the impact of those efforts. A 4,000-square-mile region incorporating 88 cities, Los Angeles County is a challenging environment in which to provide services for older people.

Trejo explained that as the third leading cause of death in Los Angeles County, Alzheimer's disease is now influencing policy, systems, and service delivery. She first highlighted an age-friendly initiative launched in 2016 that engaged more than 22 elected officials in the region and prioritized not only age-appropriateness, accessibility, and inclusiveness but also dementia-friendly components.[6]

Trejo noted that her team works continuously to help the Los Angeles County community understand how to respond to the changing needs of its residents. For example, an effort that began at the regional level 3 years

---

[4] https://acl.gov/CaregiverStrategy
[5] https://www.whitehouse.gov/briefing-room/presidential-actions/2023/04/18/executive-order-on-increasing-access-to-high-quality-care-and-supporting-caregivers
[6] https://purposefulagingla.com/index.html

ago to develop a strategic plan for brain health[7] incorporates several dimensions. Given the diversity of the community, one of these dimensions is evaluating implications of health disparities among people with dementia, with particular attention to linguistic and cultural issues in service delivery, assessment, and intervention (see, e.g., previous work from Aranda et al., 2003). She indicated that Los Angeles County is also considering implementing a framework with a lifespan approach to evaluate how the county is investing its resources to improve the quality of life for its residents.

Trejo pointed out that because several different systems play a role in delivering care to people with dementia and providing support to their families, the county is increasing its cross-sector collaborations. For instance, her office collaborated with the county's public health director to begin strategic brain health planning for its aging population. As another example of effective cross-sector collaboration, she explained that her team worked with local law enforcement to launch L.A. Found,[8] an intervention that provides global positioning system tracking devices to family members to help locate people with dementia who have wandered from their homes.

Trejo and her team are also considering workforce opportunities in the county that could be leveraged to improve the early identification of people's medical conditions and needs (especially among minority populations) and the needs of their caregivers and thus improve the provision of care. To provide better support, especially for family caregivers, she and her team are reviewing records of who visits the emergency room and what care they receive. The goal of this effort is to improve continuity of care with better follow-up communication. For example, an emergency alert response system intervention allows families to call 911 and participate in a screening process to determine whether an emergency room visit is warranted for their loved one, and this screening call is followed up with social services and supports. She indicated that this intervention has demonstrated a decrease in the high utilization of expensive, unnecessary emergency care.

Trejo noted that community-wide education is another important goal in the county. For example, Dementia Friends LA[9] was launched by first engaging elected officials and then by creating an ambassador program throughout the community. She expressed her hope that such strategic initiatives will begin to change the way community members respond to people experiencing dementia.

Trejo underscored that implementing and measuring the effectiveness of such strategic initiatives at the local level requires support and funding from policymakers (see, e.g., Aranda et al., 2021). She urged vigilance at both the policy and program levels as the field of dementia care continues to evolve;

---

[7] http://publichealth.lacounty.gov/seniorhealth/abouthbla
[8] https://lafound.lacounty.gov
[9] https://www.alzheimersla.org/for-communities/dementia-friends

including people with dementia and their caregivers in this important work remains critical. Exciting work is ongoing at the community level, she continued, including collaborations with universities and other research partners, to document this work and expand the field. She stressed that these partnerships create a key opportunity for underserved populations to be included in research.

DISCUSSION

Sharing questions from workshop participants, Amy Kind (Associate Dean for Social Health Sciences and Programs at the University of Wisconsin–Madison; planning committee member), moderated a discussion among the session's three speakers. She invited each to discuss an important research opportunity to improve social services, connectivity, and support networks for people with dementia and their families.

Trejo urged NIA to examine how Alzheimer's Demonstration Grants have affected systems of care in the communities that received them. Fabius highlighted the lack of data available on the direct care workforce, especially on a statewide or national scale, which makes formulating key research questions and providing meaningful recommendations for family caregivers very difficult. Shah noted that more research is needed to develop strategies to support older people living with dementia and their care partners as acute illness develops and dementia evolves—without going to EDs.

Kind asked Shah to describe the responsibilities of community paramedics, especially when they encounter people with dementia who live alone. Shah reiterated that a community paramedic's primary goal is to avoid transporting the person to the hospital—for example, by repairing a person's laceration in the home. He advocated for the development of a support structure specifically for people who live alone to ensure that they are not putting themselves at increased risk.

In response to Kind's observation that social isolation is a crosscutting theme of the workshop, Fabius explained that she found low levels of social engagement for older people in general in her research and noted that social engagement and social isolation are important measures of quality of care. She stressed that having a person in one's house does not guarantee *meaningful* engagement; further research could help determine how HCBS could best address such social engagement issues. Trejo described a policy position adopted by the Board of Supervisors in Los Angeles County that focuses on the importance of social connectedness. Approximately 30 county departments are working together to determine what each can do to improve the "social fabric" of the community—for example, by embracing the role of culture in improving health access and wellness among older adults.

Emily Agree (Research Professor and Associate Director, Hopkins Population Center, Johns Hopkins University; planning committee chair) asked about the role of language in service delivery to communities. Trejo responded that appropriate language skills are incredibly important to providing quality care; when people are in distress, they often communicate in their native language. To provide the best care, she championed the use of peer-support strategies as a way to educate and empower both communities and older adults, and she suggested adding professionals with language skills to a community's support networks instead of asking families to have their own interpreters. She added that professionals who speak another language need to be recognized and rewarded for the value they provide to their communities.

Fabius agreed that language skills are highly valuable. For example, she said, people should not have to travel exceptionally long distances just to find an adult day center with staff who speak their language. Similarly frustrating situations arise in nursing home settings when only one staff person speaks the native language of a resident, causing the resident to feel isolated. Fabius emphasized that if agencies began to compensate staff appropriately for critical language and communication skills, language barriers could be addressed and high turnover rates of paid care positions could be decreased. Shah remarked that language barriers are also a significant challenge in emergency medicine, especially given the limited diversity among clinicians and paramedics. He underscored that in addition to speaking the language, being part of the community and the culture is essential; for example, when people from rural areas serve as paramedics in their communities, this builds trust and capacity and improves job fulfillment.

Wendy Rogers (Khan Professor of Applied Health Sciences, University of Illinois Urbana-Champaign; planning committee member) inquired about the best strategies for providing dementia training to paid caregivers, paramedics, and other support workers. Fabius noted that only 14% of home care agencies surveyed in Maryland require dementia-specific training, even though most of their clients have dementia. She said that additional evidence needs to be developed and then communicated to demonstrate how increased dementia training, tailored to the unique settings of assisted living and personal residences, improves both care delivery and caregiver knowledge. She highlighted another challenge in that without any national requirements for training, training is at the state's or specific agency's discretion, and decisions are affected by cost and staff availability.

Shah noted that because paramedics and ED staff already have so much training to complete, adding dementia-specific training is a challenge. However, building a community paramedic program focused specifically on people with dementia would reduce the number of people who need this training. He stressed that further research is needed to determine key competencies and milestones as well as evaluation measures for such training.

Trejo suggested first identifying the workforce that needs to be trained and then determining the minimum amount of training needed for that workforce to perform appropriately. When the training is focused properly, she continued, the workforce is more likely to complete it. For example, in her role to develop protocols for frontline clinical staff who need to acquire a new skill, she reviews validated standard instruments and adapts them as appropriate for the applied setting to train the workforce.[10]

Reflecting on another crosscutting theme of the workshop, the importance of cross-sector collaboration, Kind asked what critical research and infrastructure investment are needed to improve connectivity across siloed community systems. Trejo observed that no shared definition of terms exists across agencies, which creates stress for families and those trying to create programs for the community. She advocated for developing a standard lexicon at the federal level across systems, which would also improve data alignment. To improve cross-sector collaboration further, she said, dedicated leadership for improving care of people aging with dementia is needed at the community level.

Fabius discussed the role of embedded pragmatic clinical trials in facilitating collaborative efforts; these efforts could help overcome the issues that arise when people work in silos and neither the data nor the people talk to one another, resulting in the same findings. Shah added that the EMS system has always operated within a silo: it has a massive amount of information but no way to communicate it with other service agencies or health systems. Without this capability, he continued, providing the holistic and comprehensive support that people, especially older people with dementia, need is not possible.

Kind posed a question about how to support this research and practice on a fiscal level. Trejo advocated for increased partnership between those in applied settings and those in academia. She encouraged community leaders to "shop their questions around" the research community, find someone who can help answer them, and then provide justification to a policymaker for financing. Because making such connections is sometimes difficult, she suggested that the research community initiate partnerships as well. Shah urged researchers to think more broadly about important outcome measures for community programs and identified the challenge of crossing social and medical service domains, which have unique complexities in measuring cost and best supporting activities. He also championed increased partnerships, noting that academic institutions welcome and often seek out collaborative opportunities with community groups. Fabius agreed that partnership is key to moving the field forward, and she "keeps her ear to the street" to understand what critical questions need to be answered for the community. She also indicated that Medicaid HCBS could learn lessons from how states used American Rescue Plan Act funds (e.g., expanding services, reducing waiting lists) and which strategies worked best.

---

[10] https://file.lacounty.gov/SDSInter/dmh/159942_the_oa_geriatric_field_screening_protocol.pdf

SUMMARY OF WORKSHOP DAY 2

In closing the discussion, Elena Fazio (Director of the Office of Alzheimer's Disease and Alzheimer's Disease-Related Dementias Strategic Coordination in the Division of Behavioral and Social Research, NIA) identified themes that emerged during the second day of the workshop: (a) the importance of focusing more specifically on people with dementia aging in place or in the community; (b) the need to focus on workforce training and availability; (c) the value of both collective and individual services for people with dementia aging in place; (d) the exploration of what it means to live where you want to live, with consideration of how that choice is made and who can make it; (e) recognition of the disparities in health care access; and (f) an understanding of how housing interacts with aging in place and beyond. Fazio also mentioned a new NIA funding opportunity for a state dementia care research center that will focus on dementia care practices, policies, and programs that are working at the state and substate levels.

Agree followed with a summary of her key takeaways from the third and fourth sessions of the workshop. She noted that several speakers discussed strategies to evaluate successful programs for aging in place for people with dementia, building on previous workshop conversations about the ambiguous concept of place and the fact that some people want to stay in the homes in which they have always lived while others are "trapped" in unmanageable environments. Thus, some speakers highlighted the concept of "aging in the right place," a perspective that may change as dementia progresses and as family resources and needs evolve. She noted that speakers explained that understanding the triggers that indicate that people with dementia and their families need more assistance is a key component to adapting environments to people.

Agree mentioned that one speaker described the critical role of paid care workers and how much they improve the experiences for unpaid family members providing and managing care; however, too little is known about the direct workforce and its challenges. Innovative strategies could improve information exchange between workers, families, and systems, as well as coordination of care.

Agree also observed that several speakers commented on how unaffordable housing affects one's ability to pay for necessities (e.g., care, medicine, food), and a home's inaccessibility limits social engagement. In light of these concerns, many speakers noted that policies need to be examined more closely, as housing and health policies are rarely coordinated.

Agree noted that a few speakers emphasized that research on dementia-friendly community initiatives should build capacity for evaluation into the intervention design. Furthermore, to be sustainable, they suggested that programs not begin without assessing the resources in a community, as well as the benefits of investing in those communities.

Lastly, Agree reported that speakers also discussed social and other supportive service environments, highlighting opportunities for coordination and identifying unique resources in communities that can help facilitate aging in place with dementia. For example, an opportunity exists to better leverage paramedics to improve transitions between settings and to avoid transporting people to emergency rooms through education and delivery of acute care services. Other opportunities include the potential to set up 911 screening to notify social services of an emergency room visit. A few speakers discussed the importance of cross-sector collaborations and the potential benefits of involving other community systems in working with social service and supportive programs.

REFERENCES

Aranda, M. P., Kremer, I. N., Hinton, L., Zissimopoulos, J., Whitmer, R. A., Huling Hummel, C., Trejo, L., & Fabius, C. (2021). Impact of dementia: Health disparities, population trends, care interventions, and economic costs. *Journal of the American Geriatrics Society*, 69(7), 1774–1783. https://doi.org/10.1111/jgs.17345

Aranda, M. P., Villa, V. M., Trejo, L., Ramírez, R., & Ranney, M. (2003). El Portal Latino Alzheimer's Project: Model program for Latino caregivers of Alzheimer's disease-affected people. *Social Work*, 48(2), 259–271. https://doi.org/10.1093/sw/48.2.259

Beck, A. P., Jacobsohn, G. C., Hollander, M. M., Gilmore-Bykovskyi, A. L., Werner, N., & Shah, M. N. (2020). Features of primary care practice influence emergency care-seeking behaviors by caregivers of persons with dementia: A multiple-perspective qualitative study. *Dementia*, 20(2), 613–632.

Cornell, P. Y., Zhang, W., Smith, L., Fashaw, S., & Thomas, K. S. (2020). Developments in the market for assisted living: Residential care availability in 2017. *Journal of the American Medical Directors Association*, 21(11), 1718–1723.

Fabius, C. D., Millar, R., Geil, E., Stockwell, I., Diehl, C., Johnston, D., Gallo, J. J., & Wolff, J. L. (2023). The role of dementia and residential service agency characteristics in the care experiences of Maryland Medicaid home and community-based service participants and family and unpaid caregivers. *Journal of Applied Gerontology*, 42(4), 627–638.

Fabius, C. D., Okoye, S. M., Mulcahy, J., Burgdorf, J., & Wolff, J. L. (2022). Associations between use of paid help and care experiences among Medicare-Medicaid enrolled older adults with and without dementia. *The Journals of Gerontology: Series B*, 77(12), e216–e225.

Fabius, C. D., Okoye, S. M., Wu, M. M. J., Jopson, A. D., Chyr, L. C., Burgdorf, J., Ballreich, J., Scerpella, D., & Wolff, J. L. (2023). The role of place in person- and family-oriented long-term services and supports. *The Millbank Quarterly*, 101(4), 0728.

Fabius, C. D., Wec, A., Abshire-Saylor, M., Smith, J. M., Gallo, J. J., & Wolff, J. L. (2023). "Caregiving is teamwork...": Information sharing in home care for older adults with disabilities living in the community. *Geriatric Nursing*, 54, 171–177. https://doi.org/10.1016/j.gerinurse.2023.09.001

Fabius, C. D., Wolff, J. L., & Kasper, J. D. (2020). Race differences in characteristics and experiences of Black and White caregivers of older Americans. *The Gerontologist*, 60(7), 1244–1253.

Fashaw-Walters, S., Rahman, M., Gee, G. C., Mor, V., White, M., & Thomas, K. (2022). Out of reach: Inequities in the use of high-quality home health agencies. *Health Affairs, 41*(2), 247–255.

Feng, Z., Coots, L. A., Kaganova, Y., & Wiener, J. M. (2014). Hospital and ED use among Medicare beneficiaries with dementia varies by setting and proximity to death. *Health Affairs, 33*(4), 683–690.

Freedman, V. A., & Spillman, B. C. (2014). Disability and care needs among older Americans. *Milbank Quarterly, 92*(3), 509–541.

Garfield, R., Musumeci, M. B., & Reaves, E. L. (2015). *Medicaid's Role for People with Dementia.* KFF. https://www.kff.org/medicaid/issue-brief/medicaids-role-for-people-with-dementia

Gillespie, S. M., Wasserman, E. B., Wood, N. E., Wang, H., Dozier, A., Nelson, D., McConnochie, K. M., & Shah, M. N. (2019). High-intensity telemedicine reduces emergency department use by older adults with dementia in senior living communities. *Journal of the American Medical Directors Association, 20*(8), 942–946.

Gorges, R. J., Sanghavi, P., & Konetzka, R. T. (2019). A national examination of long-term care setting, outcomes, and disparities among elderly dual eligibles. *Health Affairs, 38*(7), 1110–1118.

Hwang, U., Carpenter, C., Dresden, S., Dussetschleger, J., Gifford, A., Hoang, L. Y., Leggett, J., Nowroozpoor, A., Taylor, Z., Shah, M. N., & GEAR and GEAR 2.0 Networks. (2022). The Geriatric Emergency Care Applied Research (GEAR) network approach: A protocol to advance stakeholder consensus and research priorities in geriatrics and dementia care in the emergency department. *BMJ Open, 12*(4), e060974.

Jacobsohn, G. C., Hollander, M., Beck, A. P., Gilmore-Bykovskyi, A., Werner, N., & Shah, M. N. (2019). Factors influencing emergency care by persons with dementia: Stakeholder perceptions and unmet needs. *Journal of the American Geriatrics Society, 67*(4), 711–718.

Joynt Maddox, K. E., Chen, L. M., Zuckerman, R., & Epstein, A. M. (2018). Association between race, neighborhood, and Medicaid enrollment and outcomes in Medicare home health care. *Journal of the American Geriatrics Society, 66*(2), 239–246.

Kasper, J., Freedman, V., Spillman, B., Wolff, J. (2015). The disproportionate impact of dementia on family and unpaid caregiving to older adults. *Health Affairs 34*(10), 1642–1649.

LaMantia, M. A., Stump, T. E., Messina, F. C., Miller, D. K., & Callahan, C. M. (2016). Emergency department use among older adults with dementia. *Alzheimer Diseases and Associated Disorders, 30*(1), 35–40.

Parker, L. J., & Fabius, C. (2022). Who's helping whom? Examination of care arrangements for racially and ethnically diverse people living with dementia in the community. *Journal of Applied Gerontology, 41*(12).

PHI. (2022). *Direct care workers in the United States: Key facts.* https://www.phinational.org/resource/direct-care-workers-in-the-united-states-key-facts-3

Reckrey, J. M., Boerner, K., Franzosa, E., Bollens-Lund, E., & Ornstein, K. A. (2021). Paid caregivers in the community-based dementia care team: Do family caregivers benefit? *Clinical Therapeutics, 43*(6), 930–941.

Reckrey, J. M., Morrison, R. S., Boerner, K., Szanton, S. L., Bollens-Lund, E., Leff, B., & Ornstein, K. A. (2020). Living in the community with dementia: Who receives paid care? *Journal of the American Geriatrics Society, 68*, 186–191.

Reckrey, J. M., Watman, D., Tsui, E. K., Franzosa, E., Perez, S., Fabius, C. D., & Ornstein, K. A. (2022). "I am the home care agency": The dementia family caregiver experience managing paid care in the home. *International Journal of Environmental Research and Public Health, 19*(3), 1311.

Shah, M. N. (2006). The formation of the emergency medical services system. *American Journal of Public Health, 96*, 414–423.

Shah, M. N., Jacobsohn, G. C., Jones, C. M. C., Green, R. K., Caprio, T. V., Cochran, A. L., Cushman, J. T., Lohmeier, M., & Kind, A. J. H. (2022). Care transitions intervention reduces ED revisits in cognitively impaired patients. *Alzheimer's & Dementia: Translational Research & Clinical Interventions, 8*(1).

Shippee, T. P., Fabius, C. D., Fashaw-Walters, S., Bowblis, J. R., Nkimbeng, M., Bucy, T. I., Duan, Y., Ng, W., Akosionu, O., & Travers, J. L. (2022). Evidence for action: Addressing systemic racism across long-term services and supports. *Journal of the American Medical Directors Association, 23*(2), 214–219.

Travers, J. L., Rosa, W. E., Shenoy, S., Bergh, M., & Fabius, C. D. (2023). Characterizing caregiving supportive services use by caregiving relationship status. *Journal of the American Geriatrics Society, 71*(5), 1566–1572.

Yeboah-Korang, A., Kleppinger, A., & Fortinsky, R. H. (2011). Racial and ethnic group variations in service use in a national sample of Medicare home health care patients with type 2 diabetes mellitus. *Journal of the American Geriatrics Society, 59*(6), 1123–1129.

6

Social Isolation and Engagement

Key Points Highlighted by Presenters

- To better support older people with dementia who do not have family and friends available, intervention development could be strengthened by increasing measures of social isolation, identifying those in need before the intervention, considering upstream factors when determining who to target and when, using a menu of solutions with a person–place focus to meet individual needs, and developing group-based and purpose-oriented strategies. (**CUDJOE**)

- Pragmatic trials and adaptive intervention designs are valuable approaches that extend beyond randomized controlled trials. Additionally, home- and community-based organizations could be used as test beds to optimize interventions before launching randomized controlled trials, as long as training protocols are developed to support community-based implementation by these organizations. (**MUDAR**)

- For those with impaired mental capacities, the usual assumption is that a family member will be available to serve as a surrogate decision maker. However, there are older adults who either do not have a suitable family member to make decisions on their behalf or do not want their family members to make decisions for them. Moreover, surrogates are, by default, expected to know how to make decisions on someone else's behalf, which is particularly difficult for questions about aging in place for people with dementia. (**COHEN**)

The fifth session of the workshop was moderated by William Vega (Distinguished Professor and Senior Scholar for Community Health, Florida International University; planning committee member), who reminded participants that the overall goal of the workshop is to identify outstanding issues to advance knowledge for intervention development. He noted that without a heuristic to assess the impact of social determinants on health, understanding the processes of effective intervention and the ability to carry out the role of caregiving is difficult (for example, see Aranda et al., 2023). He posited that validated qualitative and quantitative standardized assessment tools for use in intervention development are needed to assess the impact of these social determinants.

Vega indicated that this session of the workshop would explore issues of social isolation and social engagement for those aging in place with dementia. He explained that when individuals progressively fail in their competence to manage their environments, they may become socially isolated. Furthermore, when dementia onset occurs in the last segment of the life course, it is often accompanied by other health and mobility issues that may affect social engagement. He commented that older people living with dementia are at greater risk than others for social isolation, and having little or no support may have serious consequences for their ability to remain in their communities.

For this session, speakers and workshop participants had been asked to discuss the following questions: How are people living with dementia vulnerable to risks of isolation? What individual- and community-level factors improve or worsen the consequences of isolation for people living with dementia? What interventions are available that might be useful to support those without family or friends available?

ADDRESSING SOCIAL ISOLATION

Thomas Cudjoe (Robert and Jane Meyerhoff endowed Professor and Assistant Professor of Medicine and Nursing, Johns Hopkins University) began his presentation by sharing personal anecdotes related to issues of social isolation and engagement among older adults. He emphasized that environment and culture are important factors in people's trajectories and also that there are mutual benefits for older adults and those who are supporting them. For example, he said, when he was a medical student he rented a room from an older woman: he gained shelter, and she gained financial support, a sense of safety, ongoing social connection, and new experiences. Carefully balancing the autonomy and safety of older people and those around them is a critical piece of the discussion on social isolation and aging in place. For instance, when providing home-based primary care for a homebound older couple "aging in place," he witnessed many safety challenges (e.g., leaving the stove on during the winter for warmth) and hoarding issues, which also negatively affected the couple's neighbors.

Before exploring these issues in greater depth, Cudjoe provided a definition of social isolation: objectively having few social relationships, social roles, and group memberships, and having infrequent social interactions (Badcock et al., 2022; Holt-Lunstad, 2018). He emphasized that social isolation differs from loneliness, which is a *subjective feeling* of isolation. Social isolation includes low levels of social contact, may be chosen owing to a preference for solitude, and is not necessarily unpleasant; loneliness emerges from a mismatch between actual and desired relationships and may result in feelings of emotional distress and a low sense of control or choice. He explained that a framework for social connection considers the structure (e.g., marital status, social networks, social integration, living alone, social isolation), function (e.g., received support, perceived social support, perceived loneliness), and quality (e.g., marital quality, relationship strain, social inclusion or exclusion) of social connections and how these elements affect individuals who are living with cognitive impairment (Holt-Lunstad, 2018).

Cudjoe stressed that additional research is needed to better support older people who may be experiencing social isolation or loneliness. For example, a report recommended developing a more robust evidence base, as well as translating research into health care practice, improving awareness, strengthening education and training, and optimizing ties between the health system and community networks and resources (National Academies of Sciences, Engineering, and Medicine, 2020). More recently, the U.S. Surgeon General (2023) released an advisory on the healing effects of social connection and community; it also recommended the need to deepen knowledge so as to better address social isolation and loneliness.

Careful measurement and identification of individuals who experience social isolation and loneliness is a critical first step, Cudjoe said (for example, see Pomeroy, Mehrabi, et al., 2023). He underscored that social isolation is widespread among older adults: 25% of those aged 65 and older experience social isolation (Cudjoe et al., 2020). He also noted that experiences of social isolation may change over time (Cudjoe, 2023). Social isolation also matters at the cellular level, indicated by an elevation of inflammatory markers (Cudjoe et al., 2021).

Cudjoe pointed out that research over several decades has considered how upstream factors affect cognition (for example, see Berkman et al., 2000). More recently, scholars have begun to study the relationship between social connections and health conditions that could lead to hospitalizations and living in a nursing home (Pomeroy, Cudjoe et al., 2023). Many studies (Evans et al., 2019; National Academies, 2020) have found that social isolation increases risk for dementia in particular: for example, Huang et al.

(2023) found that socially isolated older adults have a 27% higher chance of developing dementia than other older adults over time.

However, challenging the workshop session's framing, Cudjoe indicated that few studies have examined whether older people living with dementia are at greater risk than other older adults for social isolation. He argued that not enough data from people living with dementia are available to make that assertion, and more research is needed to understand the social connections of people living with dementia. He said it is even possible that dementia could increase social connection as a result of the increased use of clinical and community-based services and family and community supports. Of course, dementia could also decrease social connection because of memory challenges related to maintaining connection; the compounding risk of poor health and function; stigma, stress, fear, anxiety, and misunderstanding; and communication issues. He underscored that research to understand this relationship is complex because of the heterogeneity of individual and community resources, challenges in diagnosis and care of people living with dementia, and the evolution in individuals' cognition over time. He said that additional work to understand the bidirectional relationship between social isolation and health conditions would be valuable.

Reflecting on one of the session's guiding questions about how people living with dementia are vulnerable to the risks of isolation, Cudjoe noted that people living with dementia may live alone and experience safety and memory challenges; have trouble performing activities of daily living; experience difficulty taking medications and going to medical appointments; struggle to obtain adequate food, water, shelter, and clothing; or be victims of elder mistreatment. Responding to the question about factors that improve or worsen the consequences of isolation for people with dementia, he said that individual-level factors include each person's life course, demographic factors, personality, and preferences; and community-level factors include housing arrangements, transportation, networks of support, and social infrastructure (e.g., senior centers and cafes). Finally, considering the question about what interventions are available to support those without available or willing family and friends, he highlighted that intervention development could be strengthened with more measures of social isolation; identification of those in need before the intervention; consideration of upstream factors when determining who to target and when; use of a menu of solutions with a person–place focus to meet individual needs; and group-based and purpose-oriented strategies.

In concluding his presentation, Cudjoe presented four approaches to addressing social isolation among older people living with dementia: (1) use the Educate, Assess, Respond framework (Holt-Lunstad & Perissinotto, 2023); (2) create easy, adaptable, and sustainable solutions; (3) start proximally;

and (4) adopt the *sawubona*[1] ("I see you") mentality. He emphasized the need to balance personal, clinical, and population perspectives; expand awareness; improve measurement; invest in research and intervention development; center equity and justice at the core of efforts; and realize assets instead of focusing solely on the deficits of people with dementia.

TECHNOLOGY TO SUPPORT SOCIAL ENGAGEMENT

Raksha Mudar (Professor of Speech and Hearing Science, University of Illinois Urbana-Champaign) emphasized that although loneliness and social isolation—two key metrics of social health—are moderately correlated, they are not the same. Reiterating the point of the previous speaker, she stressed that people who are socially isolated might not be lonely, and people who are lonely might not be socially isolated. She noted that physical, cognitive, and emotional health are affected by both social isolation and loneliness, which may alter people's quality of life.

Mudar underscored that older adults are at an increased risk of both social isolation and loneliness and their negative consequences. She explained that data from general population–based studies show that social isolation and loneliness increase the risk of developing cognitive impairment. However, because the relationship between social health and cognitive health in populations known to be at risk of dementia is not well understood, key research questions remain: Are social isolation or loneliness related to accelerated cognitive decline in populations known to be at risk of dementia (i.e., those with mild cognitive impairment and older caregivers of people with dementia)? How do other modifiable risk factors (e.g., hearing or vision loss) mediate or moderate the relationship between social health and cognitive health in at-risk populations? She said that understanding these issues could lead to the development of more targeted approaches to delay the progression of cognitive impairment and allow people to be better able to age in place.

Mudar indicated that social engagement—that is, participation in social activities and maintenance of social connections—is a key target to address isolation and loneliness in older adults. Social engagement includes both structural elements (e.g., network size) and functional elements (e.g., purpose and belonging). To better inform assessments of social engagement and guide intervention design, she advocated for developing more integrated frameworks of social engagement. For example, Lydon et al. (2022) developed a multidimensional framework that represents social activity and the social network as two interrelated dimensions that include the structural

---

[1] Traditional Zulu greeting: https://exploringyourmind.com/sawubona-african-tribe-greeting/

and functional components. This framework also represents the role of contextual and health factors in social engagement: see Figure 6-1.

Mudar explored the use of technology-based interventions to offer social engagement opportunities for older adults in the comfort of their home environments. She noted that video technology platforms, in particular, enable relatively natural opportunities for social engagement. However, accommodating the unique technology requirements and socialization needs of older adults is critical in the success of such interventions. Nie et al. (2020) published design guidance for using video technology platforms to support social engagement interventions for older adults,[2] which is based on the team's redesign of the OneClick platform to optimize use for older adults with and without mild cognitive impairment.

Mudar elaborated on the research of her team. They conducted a randomized controlled trial of the efficacy of a social engagement intervention delivered using the optimized OneClick technology platform. The goal of the intervention was to provide opportunities for older adults to connect with others, attend to social needs, reflect with others casually, and engage with others on topics of shared interest. To achieve these outcomes, she explained that collaboration with content development experts was key to ensure that the content was curated carefully for the participants: The content needed to be engaging, lead to casual conversation, lead to positive reminiscing, be accessible, capture diversity, and cater to a wide audience. Sixty different topics were developed across five broad content areas: arts and culture; nature, health, and wellness; life experiences; science and technology; and recreation and sports. The structure of the events for social interaction also had to be carefully curated to create a shared framework for conversation for the participants. After instructions from the host of the event, participants engaged in conversation in breakout rooms, with discussion prompts available as needed.

As part of the trial, 99 participants were initially divided into an intervention group and a waitlist group that began after 8 weeks. Before beginning the intervention, participants received extensive, customized technology training, and live technology support was available throughout the intervention. Even for such problems as a dropped internet connection, participants could call technology support for assistance, which motivated them to continue participating. She underscored that hiring and training the right type of technology support staff, with the ability to walk people through instructions over the phone clearly and patiently, is critical.

Mudar explained that participants were asked to attend two events per week, based on the topics of greatest interest to them and their preferred

---

[2] Dodge et al. (2015) and Yu et al. (2021) examine other technology interventions to support social interactions among at-risk individuals.

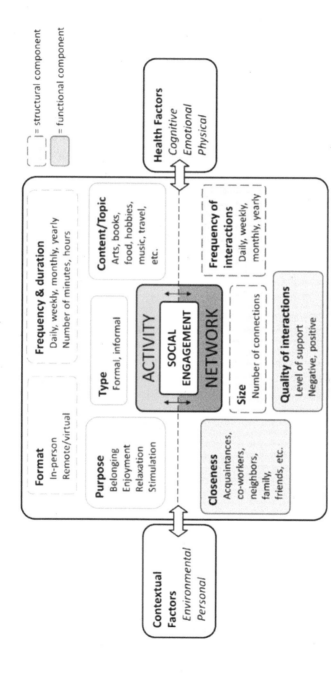

FIGURE 6-1 A framework of social engagement.
SOURCE: Lydon et al. (2022, Figure 1). Reprinted with permission.

time frames. Preliminary results of the trial revealed that participants with and without mild cognitive impairment were able to use the technology platform successfully to engage with one another, enjoyed the variety of conversation topics offered, found pretraining to be helpful, did not view occasional technology issues as a barrier to participation, and expressed interest in continuing to use the platform after the study. Home- and community-based organizations also expressed interest in using the platform to support their programs. Qualitative and quantitative analyses are ongoing to explore the efficacy of the intervention to support social engagement and quality of life. She explained that the scope of the study is being expanded to other populations, including care partners of people with dementia, 61 of whom are participating in a social engagement intervention, delivered via Zoom, designed to suit their needs for respite.

In closing, Mudar discussed the scalability issues of social engagement interventions delivered using technology. She emphasized that although one-on-one technology-based social engagement interventions target the individual needs of older adults, this approach is resource intensive. Group-based social engagement interventions using technology are more easily scalable and not as resource intensive, but they need to be designed carefully to meet individuals' varied needs, interests, and technology abilities. She pointed out that having flexible technology platforms is critical to support and scale any social engagement intervention. Developing training protocols to support the use of technology by users with varying proficiency is also essential. Beyond randomized controlled trials, she continued, pragmatic trials and adaptive intervention designs could be considered. Home- and community-based organizations could be used as test beds to optimize interventions before launching randomized controlled trials, but training protocols to support community-based implementation by home- and community-based organizations need to be developed. Finally, she emphasized the need to identify the minimum intervention dose that yields maximum benefits before increasing the reach of interventions.

SOCIAL ISOLATION AND SURROGATE DECISION MAKING

Andrew Cohen (Assistant Professor of Internal Medicine and Geriatrics, Yale School of Medicine, Yale University) defined decision-making capacity as the ability to understand the risks and benefits of a decision, reason through them, and communicate a decision about oneself. Health care professionals often speak to patients about situations in which their capacity to make decisions could be diminished as a result of a catastrophic illness, injury, or surgery, and a surrogate would be needed to make decisions on behalf of that person. This paradigm is also relevant for people with certain types of chronic disease. Many of these patients have full capacity to make and express decisions and participate in advanced care planning (preferences for which evolve over time as they adapt to their illness) until a serious illness arises close to the end of their lives, at which point a surrogate may be needed to make decisions.

In contrast, however, Cohen stressed that dementia creates a fundamentally different paradigm for decision-making capacity. The capacity to make decisions declines much more slowly over time as impairment increases, evolving from full capacity, to supported decision making, to a need for a surrogate to make decisions about housing and end-of-life decisions: see Figure 6-2.

Cohen explained that this paradigm for decision-making capacity among older people with dementia implicitly assumes that the surrogate will be a family member. Many appointed health care proxies are family members, and most states have default surrogate statutes that allow family members to make decisions for an impaired person in the absence of an official health care proxy. However, using data from a nationally representative study of older adults without dementia, Cohen et al. (2020) showed that 8% of older Americans do not have a desired surrogate. Among that 8% of older Americans, 3% had no nuclear family or confidantes; 8% had no nuclear family but did have confidantes; and 89% had nuclear family and confidantes, but they were not desired as surrogates. Therefore, he emphasized that this paradigm does not fit for a significant number of older people.

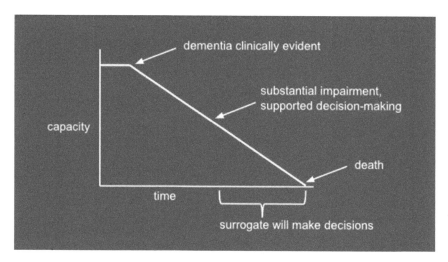

FIGURE 6-2 Decision-making capacity trajectory for older adults with dementia.
SOURCE: Workshop presentation, Andrew Cohen.

Cohen and his team are currently conducting qualitative interviews with older adults who do not have anyone in their lives whom they would select as a health care surrogate. Some participants expressed interest in completing an inverse health care proxy form, if it was available, to list people who are *not* allowed to make decisions on their behalf. Questions remain about these "unrepresented adults" who may develop impaired decision-making capacity but have no suitable surrogate. He pointed out that this is especially challenging when incapacity is prolonged, such as for people living with dementia, and the types of decisions that need to be made are many and varied. In this case, the default mechanism is guardianship, in which a probate court appoints a paid professional to make decisions on behalf of the unrepresented adult. He commented that although this approach has not been studied in depth—in part because no centralized data exist about guardianship in most states—many people find it to be a problematic option.

To study people under guardianship, Cohen and his team used Department of Veterans Affairs data, which indicated that two-thirds of people under professional guardianship live in nursing homes; fewer than half of these people have no nuclear family; professional guardians receive little training in how to make decisions for people with dementia; and, contrary to popular belief, professional guardians' medical decisions are similar to those made by family surrogates for other patients. In another study of people with advanced dementia at the end of life, Cohen et al. (2021) confirmed that professional guardianship decisions are overall about the same as decisions made by family members.

Cohen also challenged implied assumptions about surrogates, which are not only that they will be family members, but also that they know how to make decisions on someone else's behalf. This assumption about decision-making capability is especially problematic when the surrogate is an appointed professional who has no previous relationship with the person, although family members making decisions for their loved ones also have an incredibly difficult task. Surrogate decision making for people with dementia in particular is extremely difficult, especially around questions about aging in place, because the person's capacity to express preferences may diminish long before such critical decisions need to be made.

Moving forward, Cohen said, the following questions require additional exploration to address these complex issues of decision making: How and when can and should people who do not have a desired surrogate be identified? What can one do when someone does not have a desired surrogate before that person's decision-making capacity becomes impaired? How can professional guardians and other surrogates be trained to make good decisions?

DISCUSSION

Reflecting on key themes from this session of the workshop, Vega observed that understanding the vital characteristics of a support system is critical. He reiterated that social isolation may occur even among older people with caregivers, especially among those who experience aggression and behavior issues as their dementia progresses. He said that social isolation is a complex problem, owing in part to cultural and linguistic issues that could enable or hinder engagement, as well as to family dynamics that change over time. Questions remain about which interventions are best suited to which individuals, how to assess these interventions systematically, and how to select the right people for interventions and tailor their training appropriately. Additional questions remain about legal decision making, especially as it relates to the social distance of and social power in families, which could also influence the success of interventions.

With consideration for declining civic participation in the United States and the general individualistic orientation of U.S. culture, Lis Nielsen (National Institute on Aging [NIA]) asked if particular characteristics of societies or communities make them more or less likely to embrace the task of reducing social isolation among individuals living with dementia. Without attempting to make any society-level generalizations, Cudjoe cautioned that the increased political polarization in the United States could influence whether and how people engage; more research is needed to examine the broader effect of the current polarization. He highlighted several specific promising efforts to reduce social isolation, including work by the Robert Wood Johnson Foundation and activity in the Blue Zones,[3] which promote meaningful interaction.

Elena Fazio (Director of the Office of Alzheimer's Disease and Alzheimer's Disease-Related Dementias Strategic Coordination, Division of Behavioral and Social Research, NIA) invited the speakers to expand on their discussions of how people living with dementia are vulnerable to risks of isolation. Mudar replied that as these people try to understand what is happening to them, they may withdraw from their connections. For example, people beginning to experience mild cognitive impairment may avoid leaving the house and seeing other people to prevent uncomfortable situations (e.g., not remembering people's names). Cudjoe added that community-based organizations are doing good work to support the social connections of people living with dementia, but this work needs to be examined and disseminated more broadly so that more people can benefit. However, he cautioned against "overmedicalizing" the social connection aspect of aging.

---

[3] Blue Zones is an organization that uses evidence-based solutions to help people live better, longer lives; see https://www.bluezones.com

Cohen noted that people aging with dementia who do not have supportive family structures are particularly susceptible to social isolation and its negative consequences even though they may not be identified as such.

Fazio asked Cohen to elaborate on the notion of "unrepresented patients" across the range of dementia. Cohen responded that a challenge persists in the inconsistency of the terminology itself. For example, some use the term "elder orphans" to describe those who have the ability to make their own decisions but do not have a surrogate in the event that that ability is lost. However, these people are not "orphans"; they have friends who may not be the right people to serve as surrogates. He explained that people in the early stages of dementia might not be considered "unrepresented" because they are still able to make decisions; however, these people are still vulnerable to becoming unrepresented as their dementia progresses. Ideally, he continued, unrepresented adults would be identified upstream to prevent some of the issues that arise when cognitive impairment worsens. Because this level of identification is as difficult to achieve as is developing next steps to plan for this person's future, he said that further research is warranted.

Fazio expressed interest in learning more about issues specific to people with or without dementia who are aging in place alone. Cudjoe encouraged workshop participants to consult relevant research of Elena Portacolone at the University of California, San Francisco (for example, see Portacolone, 2020).

Fazio posed additional questions about technology interventions for those with cognitive impairment. She inquired about the cognitive ability of the participants in Mudar's technology-based social engagement intervention. Mudar explained that the participants had early stages of cognitive impairment. The only requirements to participate were that they had a computer or tablet that they could use with some assistance, a webcam, a quiet place, and a stable internet connection. Fazio suggested that additional research on tailoring interventions to those with more advanced stages of cognitive impairment or physical comorbidities could be helpful. Mudar agreed and highlighted another area for further exploration: information on how rural communities address issues of social isolation, and thus may face barriers in the implementation of interventions. For example, individuals in rural communities might not have access to broadband required to participate in a technology-based intervention for social engagement.

Emily Agree (Research Professor and Associate Director, Hopkins Population Center, Johns Hopkins University; planning committee chair) observed that as relatively younger cohorts age, people will have more knowledge about technology and more comfort with virtual settings. Therefore, she asked how to build sustainability into technology-based interventions for social engagement. For example, she wondered if people would be given the tools and the skills to continue communicating on their own, or if they would only be able to communicate through a specific platform. Cudjoe mentioned research on how people's use of technology affects their risk of social isolation. To sustain interventions—technology-based or otherwise—he advocated for the development of "capable" interventions that meet individuals where they are and meet their unique needs; purpose-driven, goal-oriented interventions to increase social connection are critically important.

REFERENCES

Aranda, M. P., Baier, R., Hinton, L., Peak, K. D., Jackson, J. D., Dilworth-Anderson, P., Gitlin, L. N., Jutkowitz, E., & Quiñones, A. R. (2023). Preparing for pragmatic trials in dementia care: Health equity considerations for nonpharmacological interventions. *Journal of the American Geriatrics Society.* https://doi.org/10.1111/jgs.18568

Badcock, J. C., Holt-Lunstad, J., Bombaci, P., Garcia, E., & Lim, M. H. (2022). *Position statement: Addressing social isolation and loneliness and the power of human connection.* Global Initiative on Loneliness and Connection.

Berkman, L. F., Glass, T., Brissette, I., & Seeman, T. E. (2000). From social integration to health: Durkheim in the new millennium. *Social Science and Medicine, 51*(6), 843–857.

Cohen, A. B., Costello, D. M., O'Leary, J. R., & Fried, T. R. (2020). Older adults without desired surrogates in a nationally representative sample. *Journal of the American Geriatrics Society, 69*, 114–121.

Cohen, A. B., Han, L., O'Leary, J. R., & Fried, T. R. (2021). Guardianship and end-of-life care for veterans with dementia in nursing homes. *Journal of the American Geriatrics Society, 69*(2), 342–348.

Cudjoe, T. K. M. (2023). Correlates of loneliness and social isolation in old age: Poverty. In A. Hajek, S. G. Riedel-Heller, & H.-H König (Eds.), *Loneliness and social isolation in old age.* Routledge.

Cudjoe, T. K. M., Roth, D. L., Szanton, S. L., Wolff, J. L., Boyd, C. M., & Thorpe Jr., R. J. (2020). The epidemiology of social isolation: National Health & Aging Trends Study. *Journal of Gerontology Series B: Psychological Sciences and Social Science, 75*(1), 107–113.

Cudjoe, T. K. M., Selvakumar, S., Chung, S., Latkin, C. A., Roth, D. L., Thorpe Jr., R. J., & Boyd, C. M. (2021). Getting under the skin: Social isolation and biological markers in the National Health and Aging Trends Study. *Journal of the American Geriatrics Society, 70*(2), 408–414. https://doi.org/10.1111/jgs.17518

Dodge, H. H., Zhu, J., Mattek, N., Bowman, M., Ybarra, O., Wild, K., Loewenstein, D. A., & Kaye, J. A. (2015). Web-enabled conversational interactions as a means to improve cognitive functions: Results of a 6-week randomized controlled trial. *Alzheimer's & Dementia, 1*(1), 1–12. https://doi.org/10.1016/j.trci.2015.01.001

Evans, C. J., Ison, L., Ellis-Smith, C., Nicholson, C., Costa, A., Oluyase, A. O., Namisango, E., Bone, A. E., Brighton, L. J., Yi, D., Combes, S., Bajwah, S., Gao, W., Harding, R., Ong, P., Higginson, I. J., & Maddocks, M. (2019). Service delivery models to maximize quality of life for older people at the end of life: A rapid review. *Milbank Quarterly, 97*(1), 113–175. https://doi.org/10.1111/1468-0009.12373

Holt-Lunstad, J. (2018). Why social relationships are important for physical health: A systems approach to understanding and modifying risk and protection. *Annual Review of Psychology, 69*, 437–458.

Holt-Lunstad, J., & Perissinotto, C. (2023). Social isolation and loneliness as medical issues. *New England Journal of Medicine, 388*, 193–195.

Huang, A. R., Roth, D. L., Cidav, T., Chung, S.-E., Amjad, H., Thorpe Jr, R. J., Boyd, C. M., & Cudjoe, T. K. M. (2023). Social isolation and 9-year dementia risk in community dwelling Medicare beneficiaries in the United States. *Journal of the American Geriatrics Society, 71*(3), 765–773.

Lydon, E. A., Nguyen, L. T., Nie, Q., Rogers, W. A., & Mudar, R. A. (2022). An integrative framework to guide social engagement interventions and technology design for persons with mild cognitive impairment. *Frontiers in Public Health, 9*. https://doi.org/10.3389/fpubh.2021.750340

National Academies of Sciences, Engineering, and Medicine. (2020). *Social isolation and loneliness in older adults.* The National Academies Press.

Nie, Q., Nguyen, L. T., Myers, D., Gibson, A., Kerssens, C., Mudar, R. A., & Rogers, W. A. (2020). Design guidance for video chat system to support social engagement for older adults with and without mild cognitive impairment. *Gerontechnology, 20*(1), 1–15. https://doi.org/10.4017/gt.2020.20.1.398.08

Pomeroy, M. L., Cudjoe, T. K. M., Cuellar, A. E., Ihara, E. S., Ornstein, K. A., Bollens-Lund, E., Kotwal, A. A., & Gimm, G. W. (2023). Association of social isolation with hospitalization and nursing home entry among community-dwelling older adults. *JAMA Internal Medicine, 183*(9), 955–962.

Pomeroy, M. L., Mehrabi, F., Jenkins, E., O'Sullivan, R., Lubben, J., & Cudjoe, T. K. M. (2023). Reflections on measures of social isolation among older adults. *Nature Aging,* 3(12)1463–1464.

Portacolone, E. (2020). Older Americans living alone: The influence of resources and intergenerational integration on inequality. *Journal of Contemporary Ethnography, 44*(3), 280–305.

U.S. Surgeon General. (2023). *Our epidemic of loneliness and isolation: The U.S. Surgeon General's Advisory on the healing effects of social connection and community.* https://www.hhs.gov/sites/default/files/surgeon-general-social-connection-advisory.pdf

Yu, K., Wild, K., Potempa, K., Hampstead, B. M., Lichtenberg, P. A., Struble, L. M., Pruitt, P., Alfaro, E. L., Lindsley, J., MacDonald, M., Kaye, J. A., Silbert, L. C., & Dodge, H. H. (2021). The Internet-Based Conversational Engagement Clinical Trial (I-CONECT) in socially isolated adults 75+ years old: Randomized controlled trial protocol and COVID-19 related study modifications. *Frontiers in Digital Health, 3*, 714813. https://doi.org/10.3389/fdgth.2021.714813

7

Research Implications of Community-Based Interventions and Policies

---

Key Points Highlighted by Presenters

- Implementing and sustaining effective programs for older adults with dementia to age in place is complicated by issues of inequality, a lack of affordable housing, disasters related to climate change, and funding challenges. (**SHIH**)

- Before research begins, measures about outcomes of interest need to be identified; these can be used to guide the implementation and the management of the intervention so that implementers have confidence that the adapted intervention will be successful; for tribal communities, interventions often need to be adapted to meet cultural needs. (**FINKE**)

- To support community living for people with dementia and their caregivers, research focused on strengths-based, person-centered supports and services would be beneficial; targeting people's strengths instead of deficits may result in resilience, which gives both those with dementia and their caregivers confidence and pride. (**LONG**)

- True community engagement develops by identifying a community; addressing its specific needs and wants; creating a bidirectional, integrated relationship that recognizes the community's expertise; and investing in and providing culturally appropriate, educational, credible, and meaningful resources to that community. (**GREEN-HARRIS**)

In the final session of the workshop, four speakers participated in a discussion of research that is needed to develop scalable interventions and new policies at the community level for aging in place with dementia, focused on the following questions: What research is needed to identify the challenges to implementation in real-world programs? Where is there room for innovations in delivery of services, organization of infrastructure, and supportive services? How can interventions be developed to be sustainable in diverse community settings?

HOME- AND COMMUNITY-BASED PROGRAMS

Regina Shih (Professor of Epidemiology and Health Policy and Management, Emory University, and Adjunct Policy Researcher, RAND) introduced several challenges for aging in place with dementia, including inequality, housing affordability and availability, the global threat of climate change, and the role of technology. In the context of these challenges, she described three projects that are advancing aging-in-place opportunities for older adults and people with dementia and offered directions for future research.

Shih explained that the Centers for Medicare & Medicaid Services (CMS) has been rebalancing long-term care over the past few decades to decrease costs. For example, as an alternative to nursing home settings, home- and community-based services (HCBS) support aging in place through personal care, home health, care management, and more; this support is delivered in many venues, including people's homes, senior centers, adult day care centers, and congregate meal sites. She stressed that improving the delivery of HCBS requires measures of equality, access, and cost, yet measuring HCBS is very difficult because many services, providers, and settings of care are involved. Furthermore, gaps persist in access to and tracking of HCBS utilization for people with dementia.

To address these gaps, Shih noted that the National Institute on Aging (NIA) funded the Community Care Network for Dementia (CaN-D),[1] an initiative that fosters knowledge sharing to advance innovative dementia HCBS research; generates data tools on dementia HCBS measures; expands and diversifies the group of dementia HCBS researchers; facilitates translation of research into policy; and develops network infrastructure, products, and mentorship activities through a diversity, equity, and inclusion lens. This network is led by Emory University, RAND, the University of Michigan, and the New York Academy of Medicine. Encouraging workshop participants to join CaN-D, she noted that the network currently has 250 members, including dementia and HCBS advocates, providers, researchers, federal and state agency representatives, and philanthropic organizations.

---

[1] https://sph.emory.edu/can-d

Shih provided an overview of another project, the Public Health Center of Excellence on Dementia Caregiving (PHCoE-DC).[2] This project recognizes that family caregivers are essential to supporting aging in place for their loved ones who have dementia. She stressed that the better that public health professionals can prepare caregivers for their roles, the less likely the person with dementia is to be placed in a nursing home. The Building Our Largest Dementia Infrastructure for Alzheimer's Act, passed in 2018, enables PHCoE-DC to support public health agencies in facilitating access to evidence-informed services, programs, and interventions to reduce stress and improve the health of people with dementia and their caregivers. It also provides a link to community-based healthy aging programs, caregiver education, home health care, home modification, adult day and respite care, and transportation services. She added that RAND will be assessing PHCoE-DC's ability to ensure equitable access to information and resources for family caregivers from diverse communities through public health agencies.

The final project that Shih discussed was a study on climate preparedness with villages[3] and other age-friendly communities (Shih et al., 2018). This study responds to the fact that climate-related events disproportionately affect older adults and people with dementia because they often live in vulnerable regions, have age-related comorbidities and body temperature regulation issues, and have difficulty with the stress of evacuation and displacement. She explained that (a) public health agencies focus on climate preparedness and disease prevention for the general population but do not typically target older adults, and (b) villages and (c) age-friendly communities focus on daily quality-of-life needs for aging in place but do not typically include preparedness planning. Therefore, this project, funded by the Centers for Disease Control and Prevention, better aligns the efforts among these three entities and tailors preparedness to older adults. Collaborators include RAND, the National Association of County and City Health Officials, the D.C. Department of Health, the Village to Village Network, and American Association of Retired Persons (AARP) Age-Friendly Communities. She indicated that AARP's approach is top-down, with local and regional agencies facilitating independent living of older residents through eight livability domains. The villages support aging in place with a bottom-up approach, where neighborhood grassroots organizations (usually volunteers) help older adults live at home. The United States has approximately 300 villages, for which the membership fee provides such benefits as educational seminars, services for transportation and home repairs, and social events.

---

[2] https://bolddementiacaregiving.org
[3] Typically determined by geographic areas, villages are membership organizations comprised of older adults living in their own homes that promote aging in place.

Shih remarked that the project on climate preparedness with villages and age-friendly communities resulted in the development of a toolkit (Acosta et al., 2018) on integrating activities across public health agencies, villages, and age-friendly communities. This toolkit describes aging-in-place programs as "trusted partners" for public health agencies to tailor climate preparedness activities to older adults; engages age-friendly communities and villages with a community-based participatory research approach in developing and implementing climate preparedness activities for older adults; leverages a strengths-based approach to build community resilience; and provides evaluation assistance to inform the business case for increased financial, staffing, and social support.

Reflecting on these three projects, Shih highlighted the challenges of real-world program implementation related to issues of inequality, housing, and climate change. First, villages have persistent inequalities in terms of their reach and their ability to serve members with cognitive impairment. They have been criticized for being comprised predominantly of affluent, White, older adults. Although efforts are made to reach out to people who have low-incomes as well as minorities, she said that many are not interested in a subsidized membership to such a community. Thus, villages need both assistance to reach diverse communities and to be organically grown by local communities. Faith-based and other cultural communities are joining the village movement in an effort to reach diverse adults and create new villages. With an increased number of members experiencing mild cognitive impairment, villages could better support their members with information about early detection, dementia care planning, and increased interaction with medical providers, while respecting their independence.

Second, Shih pointed out that HCBS uptake requires stable and affordable housing. Aging-in-place efforts could be conduits for raising awareness about services and eligibility for Medicaid HCBS. Because gentrification and displacement pressures may accompany people's long tenure in a neighborhood, research is under way to determine the effectiveness of intergenerational housing models and to better align housing subsidy programs with other social benefit programs, such as Medicaid HCBS. She posited that villages could also be key partners in developing pathways to community living for older adults.

Third, Shih stressed that during disasters related to climate change, early planning for and communication about timely evacuation, safe return procedures, locations of medical special needs shelters, and considerations for sheltering in place are key for people with dementia and their caregivers. Expanded partnerships and alignment between the preparedness community and dementia-friendly communities are also critical for climate change–related disasters.

Shih noted that program sustainability and scalability are additional challenges in diverse community settings. For example, 40% of villages are entirely run by volunteers, and membership dues only cover approximately 50% of operating costs—a model that is not sustainable. Moving forward, other volunteer workforces could be integrated, and partnerships could be developed with other community-based organizations and academic medical centers to leverage lower-cost providers. Microgrants from local governments could also help sustain and expand villages, she noted. In terms of scalability, the village model has experienced success when local government and philanthropy—which have a clear interest in return on investment—are involved. However, because villages take an average of 2 years to set up (involving bylaws, insurance, volunteer recruitment, etc.), some are experimenting with a quicker hub and spoke model with one main office for several villages or regional outposts.

Finally, Shih discussed innovations in service delivery. Reflecting specifically on the role of technology, she noted that two-thirds of villages now use software to book and track services with a consistent taxonomy. With this taxonomy and better data, research opportunities abound. To improve climate preparedness among older people living with dementia, she encouraged agencies to integrate their data systems. Additional research on the usability and feasibility of assistive technology for people living at home with dementia would also be valuable. The use of assistive technology for home care workers is another important avenue of exploration. Shih described significant opportunities in equitable surveillance efforts, service delivery and quality, and aging-in-place outcomes for people with dementia. She underscored that true data equity means that comprehensive data are collected and shared on race, ethnicity, and language. "Equity weighting"[4] for people with dementia is a key aspect of data equity. Dementia-specific training for aging in place programs is another critical innovation. As one example, she mentioned the AARP Dementia-Friendly America Tool, which provides online resources to create more inclusive and supportive communities for people living with dementia.

AN IMPLEMENTER'S PERSPECTIVE

Bruce Finke (Elder Health Consultant, Indian Health Service [IHS]) provided an overview of how people can use the research that is currently being conducted on services for people with dementia and frail elders and how that knowledge can inform future research design. He focused particularly on tribal communities. Finke described his work to address

---

[4] Shih defined "equity weighting" as a new way to assess health care quality by calibrating incentives to align with equity goals rather than simply closing a disparity on one dimension.

an unmet need related to palliative care services with Theresa Bowannie, director of the Zuni Home Health Care Agency (Finke et al., 2004). This tribal home health agency was certified in the state of New Mexico by CMS; however, CMS's approach to hospice had several specific features that do not align with the culture of the tribal community and could not be achieved with limited staffing and resources. Therefore, Bowannie created a palliative care program in collaboration with the IHS hospital's medical services and modeled after the Medicare hospice program. Personal care assistants were placed in homes to provide the right kind of support for tribal members in need of palliative care, and hospital resources and staff provided guidance. Although this palliative care program differed in several ways from the hospice program offered by Medicare, it still met many of Medicare's outcomes and goals. Finke emphasized that this type of adapted implementation is often valuable in tribal communities.

Finke explained that existing interventions and models (e.g., the Medicare hospice program) have been tested in pragmatic and explanatory trials, and much data on effects and outcomes are available. Often, some information about process and context is available as well. He remarked that these resources are helpful in determining whether an intervention is meeting a need that also exists in a tribal community. Then, the next step is to take that model and adapt it for and implement it in the tribal community with some degree of fidelity. He shared a definition of "fidelity" from Ginsburg et al. (2021, p. 2): "The extent to which an intervention is implemented as intended, and it provides important information regarding why an intervention may or may not have achieved its intended outcome." Implementers are faced with a question about whether they can be confident that the adapted intervention will be successful if certain changes are made. Thus, he underscored that before research begins, measures need to be identified that can be used to guide the implementation and the management of the intervention. He stressed that these measures should primarily be about achieving outcomes of interest.

Finke described intervention implementation challenges related to financial and human resource issues (e.g., availability of appropriate skill set and licensure) and other contextual issues (e.g., cultural, historical, organizational, political, population-based, geographic). For example, some of the comprehensive dementia care models are often designed for and better-suited toward those in urban areas than those in tribal communities. However, he said that the tribal communities take all of this information into account and apply it in a way to achieve the desired outcome.

Finke also pointed out that the workshop's guiding questions could be answered in different ways in different tribal communities, which creates an additional challenge for implementing interventions. Thus, the more research that is done in partnership with tribal communities, the better the data will be to drive implementation in those communities. Furthermore, he continued, because not all of the answers to these questions will come from research, another valuable knowledge-building approach is to consult with experts in tribal communities. He summarized that research in partnership with tribal and urban Indian communities generates new knowledge *through* implementation.

Finke urged implementers to understand complex or multifactorial interventions as individually validated, evidence-based practices. He described complex interventions as being comprised of building blocks that can be integrated one at a time, enabling incremental implementation with adaptation to the local tribal context. He stressed that thinking about implementation in pieces, rather than as a whole, is key from the start of the process of designing flexible interventions.

TRANSLATING SCIENCE TO PRACTICE

Erin Long (Team Lead for Alzheimer's and dementia programs, Administration on Aging, Administration for Community Living [ACL], U.S. Department of Health and Human Services) explained that ACL prioritizes helping older people age in place through three key strategies: investing in core HCBS that help them stay at home, building partnerships that leverage additional public and private resources, and promoting innovations to ensure continued effective outcomes in the future. Since 2014, ACL has funded grants to organizations (e.g., health care systems, universities, hospice care providers, tribal entities) across 45 states. Many of these grants serve diverse populations, and many have a critical focus on people with dementia who live alone, those living with intellectual disabilities and dementia, and caregivers who need support to manage challenging behaviors of people with dementia.

Long stressed that ACL does not fund work in institutional settings; it focuses only on settings in the community that provide dementia-capable supports and services (e.g., training, education, interventions) that are responsive to the needs and wants of people living with dementia and their caregivers. These supports and services are culturally competent, evidence-based, meaningful to the people in the community, educational, and accessible. She underscored that accessibility relates to creating services that people both want to and can receive. This consideration is especially important when implementing technology services, for which many people need access to devices and networks. All of these goals are achieved through research, translation of evidence-based research, implementation, and sustainability. She mentioned that work on 20 evidence-based interventions has led to countless translations of interventions that have been implemented with fidelity and sustained in other communities.

Long offered her key recommendation for structuring effective research on aging in place with dementia: include home- and community-based and long-term support service providers and community-based organizations in the research design and in the research for the program instead of merely asking these community representatives to refer people to the program after it is fully developed. She stressed that providers and organizations know the people in their communities, what they will accept and what they are willing to receive, what can be implemented reasonably, and what it will take to sustain programming.

Long indicated that to best support community living for people with dementia and their caregivers, more research should focus on strengths-based, person-centered supports and service practices. Focusing on people's strengths instead of deficits may result in resilience, which may give both those with dementia and their caregivers confidence and pride. She added that new, updated, validated evaluation tools that are strengths based are also needed. She advocated for research efforts that focus on people with dementia who live alone in a community, employee assistance programs that support family caregivers of people with dementia, the evaluation of the impact of dementia-friendly community work, and the availability and impact of respite days on both caregivers and people with dementia. Finally, Long suggested that any completed research package to support community-based implementation should include a cost analysis of expected financial and human investments, implementation tools and manuals for the interventionists and implementers, and simplified impact evaluation tools that can be used at the community level.

AN ASSET-BASED APPROACH TO COMMUNITY DEVELOPMENT

Gina Green-Harris (Director, regional Milwaukee office, Wisconsin Alzheimer's Institute) explained that the regional Milwaukee office of the Wisconsin Alzheimer's Institute has five integrated mission pillars: (1) community engagement, (2) community and professional education, (3) service, (4) advocacy, and (5) research. This vision empowers communities of color (primarily African American communities) by providing culturally specific health care services for their aging populations affected by dementia, Alzheimer's disease, and other health challenges.

Green-Harris noted that when the organization began in 2008, its primary goal was to determine how to achieve early diagnosis of Alzheimer's and dementia among African American people in the community, who are at higher risk for developing some form of dementia than White people. The organization initially leveraged a patient-centered memory clinic model from Sager et al. (2005), which looked at how physicians could diagnose dementia and how practitioners could work with social workers to coordinate diagnostic testing and collect data. However, a gap existed in care management—that is, follow-up services and family support. In conversation with the people in the community, Green-Harris and her team learned that they did not understand what dementia was, how it manifested, how to live with it, or how to care for it. Therefore, work began to develop a care management program that integrated the components of research, caregiving, and medical care for African American communities.

Green-Harris described her team's initial efforts to address disparities in Alzheimer's disease in African American communities and in African American participation in research. They created an asset-based model (Green-Harris et al., 2019) inspired by an earlier asset-based community development outreach model (Kretzmann & McKnight, 1993), with the hope of developing more research opportunities and more sustainable programs for the community.

Green-Harris described the Wisconsin Alzheimer's Institute's use of this asset-based model to achieve its five integrated mission pillars. First, achieving community engagement begins with identifying the community and addressing its specific needs and wants, as well as creating a cooperative, integrated relationship with the community. Part of this step includes adopting nonacademic terminology already familiar to the community (e.g., "memory loss" versus "Alzheimer's"). She asserted that recognizing the community as experts, investing in the community, and providing needed resources identified by the community are key to engaging and securing commitment from community members.

She emphasized the importance of "meeting people where they are" and fostering partnerships to deliver culturally appropriate education, training, and outreach programs to providers, those living with dementia, and family caregivers. These programs dispel myths and provide credible information to the community about dementia and other cognitive diseases; increase public awareness and understanding of health disparities and dementia to reduce the stigma, increase diagnoses, and improve access to good care; and increase education about the risk factors associated with Alzheimer's disease to improve awareness of the association between chronic illnesses and dementia.

Second, Green-Harris noted that the organization supports community and professional education by offering health care professionals recommendations on best practices of how to provide culturally appropriate care to effectively address patient, family, and community needs. The organization also collaborates with community, faith-based, and grassroots organizations to deliver presentations on risks for Alzheimer's disease and dementia; inform people about resources; and assist with navigation through available programs. In particular, the organization started hosting Breaking the

Silence events[5] in 2014 with health care professionals to bring community members together, help them to become lay experts on Alzheimer's disease and dementia, and give them tools to improve their care experiences and disease trajectories.

Third, Green-Harris highlighted that the organization is committed to improving service delivery (Dillworth-Anderson & Boswell, 2007; Hill et al., 2015). A staff person who is connected to a diagnostic memory clinic and works directly with providers conducts in-home memory assessments with families. This approach creates a strong rapport between the organization, the provider, and the patient, which increases medication adherence, attendance at medical appointments, and engagement. Green-Harris reiterated that all of these connections to service are provided and delivered in a culturally appropriate way. The organization's signature program is the Amazing Grace Chorus, which offers people with dementia and their caregivers the opportunity to sing and to participate in a program with support services and respite days (Mittelman & Papayannopoulou, 2018). She indicated that this program has improved mood, increased the time loved ones can stay in the home with their caregivers, and increased engagement with service delivery models and providers.

Fourth, Green-Harris championed the organization's efforts to strengthen advocacy. For example, a community advisory board provides a voice from the community, identifies and addresses barriers to research participation by underrepresented populations, supports the recruitment and retention of research participants, and serves as a conduit for supporting community-based participatory research. She mentioned that this model for participatory research has been replicated across Wisconsin in various sectors.

Finally, Green-Harris discussed the organization's approach to research. It first spent 2 years in the community building rapport and establishing relationships to help understand how the community wanted to see the research conducted and how to advance research on dementia and health disparities by actively engaging underrepresented populations in cutting-edge scientific studies. The organization is part of the Wisconsin Registry for Alzheimer's Prevention, including African Americans Fighting Alzheimer's in Midlife. She underscored that the asset-based participatory research model has made it possible to increase participation in research among African Americans and people of other ethnicities from 2% to nearly 20%.

In closing, Green-Harris offered the following next steps for researchers and research funders: rethink funding mechanisms to be more inclusive of community-based models, improve evaluation tools, increase community stakeholder engagement from the start and consider community members

---

[5] https://wai.wisc.edu/breakthesilence

as teammates, use integrated research strategies that are developed with people living with dementia and their caretakers, rethink equity and inclusion, and rethink funding for intervention and prevention models for high-risk communities using an asset-based model instead of a deficit model.

DISCUSSION

Sharing questions from workshop participants, Sarah Szanton (Dean and Patricia M. Davidson Health Equity and Social Justice Endowed Professor, Johns Hopkins University; planning committee member), moderated a discussion among the session's four speakers. She asked Shih to elaborate on the concept of equity weighting and how it has been used in applied research, especially for people with dementia. Shih explained that the application of equity weighting to health care quality is relatively new. She said that equity weighting creates a specific equity goal and allows for multiple identities to be included—for example, instead of having a general health care outcome, striving specifically to have double the positive outcomes for people who live in rural areas, people with a dementia diagnosis, and African Americans (Agniel et al., 2023).

Szanton then posed a question about strategies to address the effects of structural racism and discrimination across the life course. Finke replied that, where possible, services should be built into tribal programs so that they are more accessible. Shih highlighted NIA's study on the historical effects of redlining on dementia risk and cognition (Pohl et al., 2021). She stressed that to deliver person-centered care (including trauma-informed care and culturally competent care), as well as to remove barriers, people's experiences have to be at the forefront and it needs to be done equitably.

Szanton reflected on the value of strengths-based, person-centered models to provide services to both people living with dementia and their caregivers and suggested a shift in terminology from "caregiver burden" to "caregiver impact." A workshop participant highlighted the need to dedicate more funding to strengths-based measurement tools.

Szanton commented that although nearly one-third of people with dementia live alone, this population tends to be ignored by research and is more difficult to access for services. Green-Harris raised several important questions related to this issue: Are these people living alone because they want to or because they are isolated? How can these people be provided with the right resources? She remarked that some communities leverage their mail carriers and garbage collectors to identify people who live alone and may benefit from supportive services. However, she continued, because people cannot be forced to receive supports that they aren't ready to receive, one effective strategy is reaching people before cognitive impairment progresses to discuss what-if scenarios and make plans for supports.

Finke pointed out that ad hoc and informal supports may already be in place for people who are perceived to be "alone." Therefore, he suggested adopting the perspective that a continuum of support is available for individuals, instead of distinguishing "alone" from "not alone" to determine needed supports. Shih reiterated that being socially isolated, having low social networks, and living alone are interrelated but different constructs. She added that delivering services to people's homes helps to meet the needs of those without strong social networks.

Summarizing some of the overarching themes she observed from the workshop, Elena Fazio (Director of the Office of Alzheimer's Disease and Alzheimer's Disease-Related Dementias Strategic Coordination, Division of Behavioral and Social Research, NIA) reinforced the need to construct research that focuses on assets and strengths, as well as positive steps forward in measurement and intervention development, while prioritizing the challenging experiences of those diagnosed with dementia or cognitive impairment and their care partners. She also highlighted the connection between social engagement and the potential to age in place and echoed the need to review policies, services, and organizations that support people with dementia. Furthermore, rethinking equity and inclusion is critical. She championed the notion of multilayered support for individuals, which adds complexity when posing research questions and measuring effectiveness.

As the workshop drew to a close, she mentioned an NIA funding opportunity to establish state-level dementia care research centers to understand what works at the state and substate levels in terms of dementia care, and she encouraged applications from academic–community partnerships.[6]

REFERENCES

Acosta, J. D., Shih, R. A., Chen, E. K., Xenakis, L., Carbone, E. G., Burgette, L. F., & Chandra, A. (2018). *Building older adults' resilience by bridging public health and aging-in-place efforts*. RAND Corporation. https://www.rand.org/pubs/tools/TL282.html

Agniel, D., Cabreros, I., Damberg, C. L., Elliott, M. N., & Rogers, R. (2023). A formal framework for incorporating equity into health care quality measurement. *Health Affairs*, 42(10). https://doi.org/10.1377/hlthaff.2022.01483

Dillworth-Anderson, P., & Boswell, G. (2007). Cultural diversity and aging: Ethnicity, minorities, and subcultures. In G. Ritzer (Ed.), *The Blackwell encyclopedia of sociology* (Vol. II, pp. 898–902). Blackwell Publishing.

Finke, B., Bowannie, T., & Kitzes, J. (2004). Palliative care in the Pueblo of Zuni. *Journal of Palliative Medicine*, 7(1), 135–143.

Ginsburg, L. R., Hoben, M., Easterbrook, A., Anderson, R. A., Estabrooks, C. A., & Norton, P. G. (2021). Fidelity is not easy! Challenges and guidelines for assessing fidelity in complex interventions. *Trials*, 22(1), 372. https://doi.org/10.1186/s13063-021-05322-5

---

[6] https://grants.nih.gov/grants/guide/rfa-files/RFA-AG-24-033.html

Green-Harris, G., Coley, S. L., Koscik, R. L., Norris, N. C., Houston, S. L., Sager, M. A., Johnson, S. C., & Edwards, D. F. (2019). Addressing disparities in Alzheimer's disease and African-American participation in research: An asset-based community development approach. *Frontiers in Aging Neuroscience, 11.* https://doi.org/10.3389/fnagi.2019.00125

Hill, C. V., Pérez-Stable, E. J., Anderson, N. A., & Bernard, M. A. (2015). The National Institute on Aging health disparities research framework. *Ethnicity & Disease, 25,* 245–254.

Kretzmann, J. P., & McKnight, J. L. (1993). *Building communities from the inside out: A path toward finding and mobilizing a community's assets.* Center for Urban Affairs and Policy Research, Northwestern University.

Mittelman, M. S., & Papayannopoulou, P. M. (2018). The Unforgettables: A chorus for people with dementia with their family members and friends. *Intergenerational Psychogeriatrics, 30*(6), 779–789.

Pohl, D. J., Seblova, D., Avila, J. F., Dorsman, K. A., Kulick, E. R., Casey, J. A., & Manly, J. (2021). Relationship between residential segregation, later-life cognition, and incident dementia across race/ethnicity. *International Journal of Environmental Research and Public Health, 18*(21). https://doi.org/10.3390/ijerph182111233

Sager, M. A., Hermann, B., & La Rue, A. (2005). Middle-aged children of persons with Alzheimer's disease: APOE genotypes and cognitive function in the Wisconsin Registry for Alzheimer's Prevention. *Journal of Geriatric Psychiatry and Neurology, 18*(4), 245–249.

Shih, R. A., Acosta, J. D., Chen, E. K., Carbone, E. G., Xenakis, L., Adamson, D. M., & Chandra, A. (2018). *Improving disaster resilience among older adults: Insights from public health departments and aging-in-place efforts.* RAND Corporation. https://www.rand.org/pubs/research_reports/RR2313.html

Appendix A

Workshop Agenda

WORKSHOP ON AGING IN PLACE WITH DEMENTIA

Public Webcast

Workshop Goals: Discuss the state of knowledge and identify conceptual approaches to guide research on aging in place for people living with dementia in the United States. The workshop will emphasize community- and neighborhood-level factors that enable aging in place.

SEPTEMBER 13, 2023

12:30–1:00pm   Welcome and introductory remarks from the workshop planning committee and NIA
Emily Agree, Johns Hopkins University, workshop planning committee chair
Amy Kelley, National Institute on Aging
Elena Fazio, National Institute on Aging

SESSION 1—FRAMEWORKS FOR AGING IN PLACE WITH DEMENTIA

In this session speakers are being asked to explore how existing frameworks for aging in place can be adapted to incorporate people living with dementia. (Each presenter will have up to 20 minutes for their remarks.)

Guiding questions: How well do our models of the neighborhood and community factors which facilitate aging in place fit people living with dementia? What additional factors need to be taken into account? Are there unique challenges that differ from those of people with physical disabilities or chronic disease? How do structural sources of disadvantage affect people living with dementia in these communities?

1:00–2:30   Moderator: **Jennifer Manly,** Columbia University, workshop planning committee member
             Presenters:
             Frank Oswald, Goethe University
             AJ Adkins-Jackson, Columbia University
             Emily Greenfield, Rutgers University
             Q&A (30 minutes)

2:30–2:45   Break

SESSION 2—COMMUNITY-LEVEL BUILT ENVIRONMENT AND INFRASTRUCTURE

In this session speakers will discuss how aspects of the built environment and community infrastructure affect aging in place with dementia. (Each presenter will have up to 20 minutes for their remarks.)

Guiding questions: What aspects of infrastructure affect the ability of people living with dementia to age in place? Can public spaces, transportation systems, and architecture be made more friendly for people living with dementia? Are there differences in urban and rural communities in the features that are most important to people living with dementia?

2:45–4:15   Moderator: **Wendy Rogers,** University of Illinois Urbana-Champaign, workshop planning committee member
             Presenters:
             Jessica Finlay, University of Colorado
             Emmy Betz, University of Colorado
             Terri Lewinson, Dartmouth College
             Q&A (30 minutes)

4:15   Adjournment

SEPTEMBER 14, 2023

12:30–12:45   Virtual participants gather; brief introduction and reminder of workshop goals

SESSION 3—EVALUATING SUCCESSFUL AGING IN PLACE WITH DEMENTIA

In this session speakers are being asked to discuss how we can measure and evaluate aging in place with dementia. (Each presenter will have up to 20 minutes for their remarks.)

Guiding Questions: To what extent should the goals of programs that support aging in place with dementia be targeted to keep people in their own homes versus in a community or social environment? Can aging in place for people living with dementia be evaluated in terms of improvements in quality of life, deferring transitions to facility-based care, or other metrics?

12:45–2:15   Moderator: **Jennifer Ailshire,** University of Southern California, workshop planning committee member
Presenters:
Laura Gitlin, Drexel University
Jennifer Molinsky, Harvard University Joint Center for Housing Studies
Louise Lafortune, Cambridge University
Q&A (30 minutes)

2:15–2:30   Break

SESSION 4—SOCIAL SERVICES AND OTHER SUPPORT ENVIRONMENTS

This session will focus on the integration of services and other community resources. (Each presenter will have up to 20 minutes for their remarks.)

Guiding questions: How can local health and social service systems be incorporated into community level efforts to support people living with dementia, help them to stay in their own homes longer, and minimize adverse consequences? What is the role of physicians and other health care providers to improve quality of life and reduce hospitalization and institutionalization?

2:30–4:00   Moderator: **Amy Kind,** University of Wisconsin–
                 Madison, workshop planning committee member
                 Presenters:
                 Manish Shah, University of Wisconsin–Madison
                 Chanee Fabius, Johns Hopkins University
                 Laura Trejo, Los Angeles County Aging and Disabilities
                 Department
                 Q&A (30 minutes)

4:00   Adjournment

SEPTEMBER 15, 2023

12:30–12:45   Virtual participants gather; brief introduction and
                 reminder of workshop goals

SESSION 5—SOCIAL ISOLATION AND ENGAGEMENT

This session will explore the consequences of social isolation and engagement for aging in place with dementia. (Each presenter will have up to 20 minutes for their remarks.)

Guiding Questions: Older people living with dementia are at greater risk than others for social isolation and having little or no support can have serious consequences for their ability to remain in the community over time. How are people living with dementia vulnerable to risks of isolation? What individual and community level factors improve or worsen the consequences of isolation for people living with dementia? What interventions are available that might be useful to support those without family or friends available?

12:45–2:15   Moderator: **William Vega,** Florida International
                 University, workshop planning committee member
                 Presenters:
                 Thomas Cudjoe, Johns Hopkins University
                 Raksha Mudar, University of Illinois Urbana-Champaign
                 Andrew Cohen, Yale University
                 Q&A (30 minutes)

2:15–2:30   Break

SESSION 6—RESEARCH IMPLICATIONS OF
COMMUNITY-BASED INTERVENTIONS AND POLICIES

Panel discussion of future research that is needed to develop scalable interventions and new policies at the community level for aging in place for people living with dementia. (Each presenter will have up to 15 minutes for their remarks.)

Guiding questions: What research is needed to identify the challenges to implementation in "real world" programs? Where is there room for innovations in delivery of services, organization of infrastructure, and supportive services? How can interventions be developed to be sustainable in diverse community settings?

2:30–4:00   Moderator: **Sarah Szanton,** Johns Hopkins University, workshop planning committee member
Presenters:
Regina Shih, Emory University
Bruce Finke, Indian Health Service
Erin Long, Administration for Community Living
Gina Green-Harris, Wisconsin Alzheimer's Institute Milwaukee Office
Q&A (30 minutes)

4:00   Adjournment

Appendix B

Biographical Sketches for Workshop Planning Committee Members and Speakers

PLANNING COMMITTEE MEMBERS

EMILY M. AGREE (*Chair*, she/her/hers) is research professor at Johns Hopkins University and associate director of the Hopkins Population Center. Her research focuses on disability and long-term care, aging families, and intergenerational relationships. Agree is a member of the steering committee for the National Health and Aging Trends Study, a nationally representative longitudinal study of disability in later life. Her work has focused on the relationship of assistive technology use to disability in later life and the influence of population aging on family relationships and old-age support. Agree has served on the Population Association of America board of directors and on the editorial boards of *Demography*, the *Journal of Gerontology: Social Sciences*, and *Research on Aging*. She has an M.A. in demography from Georgetown University and a Ph.D. in sociology from Duke University. Agree is a member of the Committee on Population with the National Academies of Sciences, Engineering, and Medicine.

JENNIFER AILSHIRE (she/her/hers) is associate professor of gerontology and sociology, assistant dean of research, and associate dean of international programs and global initiatives at the University of Southern California. Her research addresses questions that lie at the intersections of social stratification, urban sociology, and the sociology of health and aging. In particular, Ailshire's research focuses on the importance of the neighborhood environment and social relationships in determining health over the life course. A consistent theme throughout her work is an interest

107

in gender, socioeconomic, racial, and ethnic inequality in health. Current projects include research on the links between air pollution and health in older adults, neighborhood determinants of racial and ethnic health disparities, and social factors associated with poor sleep. Ailshire has a Ph.D. in sociology from the University of Michigan.

AMY J. H. KIND (she/her/hers) is the inaugural associate dean for social health sciences and programs at the University of Wisconsin School of Medicine and Public Health. In this role, she oversees, creates synergies, and guides the growth of the school's current and future initiatives, policies, and programs designed to study and eliminate health disparities. She works closely with leaders in research, education, clinical, and public health realms to build capacity and ensure the advancement of health equity research. Kind is also a professor of medicine and serves as leader of the Care Research Core of the Wisconsin Alzheimer's Disease Research Center. She also is a resource for connecting basic and clinical scientists with social scientists to facilitate discoveries in social exposome research, a key area in mechanistic health disparities inquiry. Kind serves as executive director of the $400 million Wisconsin Partnership Program grant-making endowment, serves as director of the University of Wisconsin Center for Health Disparities Research, and provides oversight to the Milwaukee-based Center for Community Engagement and Health Partnerships. She has an M.D. from the University of Wisconsin School of Medicine and Public Health.

JENNIFER J. MANLY (she/her/hers) is professor of neuropsychology in the Department of Neurology at Columbia University Irving Medical Center. Her research focuses on mechanisms of inequalities in cognitive aging and Alzheimer's Disease. Manly's research team has partnered with Black and Latinx communities in New York City, and around the United States, to design and carry out investigations of structural and social forces across the life course, such as educational opportunities, racism and discrimination, and socioeconomic status, and how these factors relate to cognition and brain health later in life. Her research has been funded by the National Institutes of Health and the Alzheimer's Association. Manly has authored more than 220 peer-reviewed publications and 10 book chapters. She was the 2014 recipient of the Tony Wong Diversity Award for Outstanding Mentorship and was the recipient of the Paul Satz-International Neuropsychological Society Career Mentoring Award in 2020. Manly served on the HHS Advisory Council on Alzheimer's Research, Care, and Services, has been elected to the National Academy of Medicine, and is a member of the National Advisory Council on Aging. She completed her Ph.D. in neuropsychology at the San Diego State University/University of California, San Diego's joint doctoral program in clinical psychology. Manly is a member of the Committee on Population with the National Academies of Sciences, Engineering, and Medicine.

WENDY A. ROGERS (she/her/hers) is the Khan Professor of Applied Health Sciences at the University of Illinois Urbana-Champaign. She also serves as director of the McKechnie Family LIFE Home, director of the Health Technology Education Program, program director of Collaborations in Health, Aging, Research, and Technology, and director of the Human Factors and Aging Laboratory. Rogers's research interests include design for aging, technology acceptance, human–automation interaction, aging in place, human–robot interaction, aging with disabilities, cognitive aging, and training. Her research is funded by the National Institutes of Health through the National Institute on Aging and the National Institute of Nursing Research and the Department of Health and Human Services through the National Institute on Disability, Independent Living, and Rehabilitation Research. Rogers has a Ph.D. in psychology from the Georgia Institute of Technology.

SARAH L. SZANTON (she/her/hers) is the dean and Patricia M. Davidson Health Equity and Social Justice Endowed Professor. She holds a joint appointment in the Department of Health Policy and Management at the Johns Hopkins Bloomberg School of Public Health and the Johns Hopkins School of Medicine. Szanton's research includes improving health equity among older adults, aging in the community, the effects of financial strain on health, and structural racial discrimination and resilience. She co-developed the CAPABLE program, which has been tested in randomized trials and scaled to 45 new sites in 23 states. Szanton is a member of the National Academy of Medicine and the American Academy of Nursing, was a 2019 Heinz Award winner for the Human Condition, and is a PBS Organization's "Next Avenue Influencers in Aging." She has published more than 160 papers and has been the principal investigator on more than $20 million in grants. Szanton's work has been funded by the National Institutes of Health, the Center for Medicare & Medicaid Services Innovation Center, the Robert Wood Johnson Foundation, the John A. Hartford Foundation, the Rita and Alex Hillman Foundation, the St. David's Foundation, and the AARP Foundation. She has a Ph.D. from Johns Hopkins University.

WILLIAM A. VEGA (he/him/his) is distinguished professor and senior scholar for community health, Florida International University. He previously had appointments on the faculties of the University of California, Berkeley, the University of Southern California, and the Rutgers Medical Schools. He conducted community and clinical research on life course health, mental health and substance abuse issues, treatment development, and services in diverse regions of the United States and Latin America. In the past several years, Vega's research has focused on older adult health and functioning, and the prevention and management of dementia in low-resource populations. He has directed university research centers, is highly published and cited, and is an elected member of the National Academy of Medicine. Vega's research has been supported by multiple public and private agencies and foundations. Presently, he is conducting research on social determinants of health in vulnerable populations and implementation of supporting services during the transition from late middle age to older adulthood, domestically and globally. Vega has a Ph.D. in criminology from the University of California, Berkeley.

SPEAKERS

"AJ" ADKINS-JACKSON (she/her/hers) is a multidisciplinary community-partnered health equity researcher and assistant professor in the Departments of Epidemiology and Sociomedical Sciences in the Mailman School of Public Health at Columbia University. Her research investigates the role of structural racism on healthy aging for historically marginalized populations like Black and Pacific Islander communities. Adkins-Jackson's primary project examines the role of life course adverse community-level policing exposure on psychological well-being, cognitive function, and biological aging for Black and Latinx/a/o older adults. Her secondary project tests the effectiveness of an anti-racist multilevel pre-intervention restorative program to increase community health and institutional trustworthiness through multisector community-engaged partnerships. Adkins-Jackson is an alumna of the psychometrics doctoral program at Morgan State University, a historically Black university, and a board member of the Society for the Analysis of African American Public Health Issues.

EMMY BETZ (she/her/hers) is nationally known as a pioneer in injury prevention research, with a focus on older adults and firearm injury prevention. Her research on older driver decision making and firearm access in dementia has been funded by the National Institutes of Health. She launched the CU Firearm Injury Prevention Initiative in March 2023 to serve as a trusted community and national resource for firearm-related research and solutions. Betz's approach to injury prevention has been highly recognized, and she collaborates with academic colleagues, state agencies and communities to encourage unity in preventing firearm injuries and deaths on a national scale. She earned her bachelor's degree from Yale University and graduated from Johns Hopkins University with a medical degree and a master's in public health. Betz completed her emergency medicine residency at Beth Israel Deaconess Medical Center in Boston, where she served as chief resident and began conducting research on older drivers, firearm injury, and suicide. She is currently a professor of emergency medicine at the University of Colorado School of Medicine and a research physician at the Eastern Colorado Geriatric Research, Education, and Clinical Center of the Veterans Health Administration.

ANDREW B. COHEN (he/him/his) is an assistant professor in geriatrics at Yale School of Medicine and the VA Connecticut Healthcare System. He conducts research about health care decision making for persons living with dementia. Cohen has a particular interest in those who are unrepresented or "unbefriended" in the sense that they have diminished capacity and no suitable surrogate to make decisions on their behalf. In work funded by GEMSSTAR and Beeson awards from the National Institute on Aging, he has investigated decision making under guardianship, which is the default mechanism for addressing this issue. Cohen has received the Outstanding Junior Investigator of the Year award from the American Geriatrics Society. He earned a doctorate in English literature from the University of Oxford and a medical degree from the University of Pennsylvania.

THOMAS CUDJOE (he/him/his) is Robert and Jane Meyerhoff Endowed Assistant Professor and assistant professor of Medicine, Johns Hopkins University. He leverages community-based strategies, mixed-methods, and human-centered design to understand and address social isolation. Additionally, he has led studies that examined the prevalence of social isolation among older adults and associations between social isolation and health outcomes. His findings from a large nationally representative study indicate that social isolation has biological influences and could lead to poor health outcomes such as dementia and premature mortality—a finding of particular import since one in four community dwelling adults over age 65 are considered socially isolated. Cudjoe's work points to the importance of developing programs and interventions to address isolation among the aged. He holds an M.D. from Rutgers University's Robert Wood Johnson Medical School.

CHANEE FABIUS (she/her/hers) is an assistant professor in health policy and management at the Johns Hopkins Bloomberg School of Public Health. Her research informs aging and disability policies to reduce health care disparities and improve health equity for older adults and people with disabilities using long-term services and supports (LTSS). Fabius collaborates with communities to understand and improve how service providers, individuals, and families work together ensure equity in LTSS delivery. She received her Ph.D. in human development and family studies from the University of Connecticut.

BRUCE FINKE (he/him/his) is a family physician and geriatrician serving as elder health consultant in the Indian Health Service (IHS) and supporting the newly established IHS Alzheimer's Grant Program. Previously, as a primary care physician at the Zuni IHS hospital, he worked with Zuni Tribal programs in the development of clinical and community-based elder services. Finke has provided leadership in program and policy development in geriatrics and palliative care in the IHS and engaged with Tribes in improvement in geriatric clinical care and the development of long-term services and supports. He co-led the IHS primary care transformation initiative, Improving Patient Care, and served in a number of leadership roles in the Nashville Area of the IHS. For the last decade, Finke's time has been shared with the CMS Innovation Center as a senior advisor in the Learning and Diffusion Group, supporting the development of new payment and care models through the design of learning systems to foster innovation, accelerate performance, and generate insight into care delivery. He remains clinically active and represents the IHS on the Department of Health and Human Services' Advisory Council on Alzheimer's Research, Care, and Services.

JESSICA FINLAY (she/her/hers) is an assistant professor in the Department of Geography and Institute of Behavioral Science at the University of Colorado Boulder. She is a health geographer and environmental gerontologist who uses mixed methods to investigate how built, social, and natural environments affect health, well-being, and quality of life. In particular, Finlay focuses on aging in place and cognitive health disparities among underrepresented and underserved older adults. She also investigates impacts of the COVID-19 pandemic on neighborhood environments and health among aging Americans. Her National Institutes of Health (NIH) and National Science Foundation-funded research has received recognition including the NIH Matilda White Riley Behavioral and Social Science Honors. She received the National Alzheimer's Coordinating Center Rising Star Award and the Gerontological Society of America's Carroll L. Estes Rising Star Award. Finlay has an M.A. and Ph.D. in geography and gerontology from the University of Minnesota and completed a postdoctoral research fellowship at the University of Michigan.

LAURA N. GITLIN (she/her/hers) is a distinguished university professor, dean emerita, and founding executive director of the Age Well Collaboratory in the College of Nursing and Health Professions, Drexel University, and an adjunct research professor at Johns Hopkins School of Nursing. She is a sociologist by training and internationally recognized as an intervention scientist with continuous National Institutes of Health funding for over 35 years. Gitlin's research focuses on developing, evaluating, implementing and disseminating novel home- and community-based interventions to support aging in place and quality of life for older adults and family caregivers. Her interventions have resulted in improved physical and psychosocial outcomes, reduced mortality and health care savings. Gitlin has received various awards and select interventions and measures have been translated into different languages, adapted in various countries, and deployed in health systems and community-based programs within the United States. She has served as a member on National Academies of Sciences, Medicine, and Engineering committees including Families Caring for an Aging America and Human Factors in Home Health Care, as well as being a contributor to the decadal review of dementia care and invited speaker at summits hosted by the National Academies.

GINA GREEN-HARRIS (she/her/hers) is director of the Wisconsin Alzheimer's Institute Regional Milwaukee Office, as well as director of the University of Wisconsin's (UW's) School of Medicine and Public Health Center for Community Engagement and Health Partnerships in Milwaukee. Green-Harris has expertise in the areas of health equity, diversity and inclusion, cultural competency, leadership development, and research. She has received numerous awards and recognition for her work, including an UW–Madison Outstanding Woman of Color Award. In September 2020, she was appointed to chair the Governor's Health Equity Council. Green-Harris holds an M.B.A. from Franklin University and a B.S. from Central State University. She is currently a 4th year Ph.D. graduate student (dissertator status) at UW's Center for Health Disparities Research.

EMILY A. GREENFIELD (she/her/hers) is a professor of social work and director of the Hub for Aging Collaboration at Rutgers, The State University of New Jersey. Her scholarship seeks to bolster community-centered approaches for advancing innovation and equity in social programs for long and healthy lives. Greenfield's work has helped to accelerate 21st century models for aging in community, including age- and dementia-friendly community initiatives, housing-based supportive service programs, and village organizations. Hallmark features of her scholarship include both studying and participating in cross-sectoral partnerships on aging, as well as centering the voices of people leading on-the-ground community change efforts. Greenfield also conducts research on how social inequalities from childhood influence later life cognition and well-being. Funders of her work have included the Patient-Centered Outcomes Research Institute, National Institute on Aging, Alzheimer's Association, and philanthropic foundations. She obtained a Ph.D. in human development and family studies from the University of Wisconsin–Madison.

LOUISE LAFORTUNE (she/her/hers) is associate professor at Cambridge Public Health, University of Cambridge, and co-leads its life course and aging research pillar. She is principal investigator for the National Institute for Health Research (NIHR) School for Public Health Research and co-leads the NIHR Population Evidence and Data Science theme for the Applied Research Collaboration East of England. Lafortune's research has focused on developing the evidence base to address the manifold needs of older adults and help them retain quality of life in their communities. She currently leads a multifaceted research program on the social return on investment of Age Friendly Community initiatives. Lafortune serves on the World Health Organization's Technical Advisory Group for Measurement, Monitoring and Evaluation of the United Nation's Decade of Healthy Ageing, and recently chaired the Aging, Longevity and Health initiative of the International Alliance of Research Universities. She holds a dual Ph.D. in public health, specialized in organization of health services and epidemiology from both the Université de Montreal and Université de Paris.

TERRI LEWINSON (she/her/his) is an associate professor at The Dartmouth Institute for Health Policy and Clinical Practice. Her research focuses on the experience of home environments for people who have been marginalized—whether that may be in an extended-stay hotel, assisted-living facility, or senior housing—to gain an intimate understanding of what it's like for them to reside there. This work includes exploring the factors involved in residential mobility, or why people transition into and out of different home environments. Lewinson is a Gerontological Society of America Fellow, Health and Aging Policy Fellow, and a John A. Hartford Faculty Scholar. Other awards and honors include being named Alumna of the Year at the University of Georgia's School of Social Work and receiving the Distinguished Faculty Award from the Gerontology Institute at Georgia State University. She earned a B.A. from the University of South Carolina in developmental psychology, an M.S.W. from the University of Georgia, and a Ph.D. from the University of Georgia's School of Social Work.

ERIN LONG (she/her/hers) is an aging and disability program coordinator at the Administration on Aging (AoA) within the Administration for Community Living (ACL)—a federal agency providing support for older adults and people with disabilities. Alzheimer's programs she oversees at AoA have positively impacted the reduction of stigma towards individuals living with Alzheimer's disease and related dementia. Long's experience includes volunteering and working in nursing homes and assisted living communities, and she completed a practicum in a community living program for people living with disabilities. She holds a B.A. in sociology and an M.A. in social work.

JENNIFER MOLINSKY (she/her/hers) is a senior research associate at the Joint Center for Housing Studies of Harvard University and a lecturer in urban planning and design. She manages the Center's research on housing for older adults. Molinsky was lead author on several publications, including *The State of the Nation's Housing 2019*; *Older Households 2015–2035: Projections and Implications for Housing a Growing Population* (2016); and *Housing America's Older Adults: Meeting the Needs of an Aging Population* (2014). She speaks widely on the importance of suitable and affordable housing for America's older adults and has written about the role of housing on well-being and health in older age. Molinsky's work has also focused on housing affordability. She was a co-editor of the books *A Shared Future: Fostering Communities of Inclusion in an Era of Inequality* (2018) and *Homeownership Built to Last: Balancing Access, Affordability, and Risk After the Housing Crisis* (2014). Molinsky holds a B.A. from Yale University, a M.A. in public affairs-urban and regional planning from the Woodrow Wilson School at Princeton, and a Ph.D. in urban planning from Massachusetts Institute of Technology.

RAKSHA MUDAR (she/her/hers) is a professor of speech and hearing science at the University of Illinois Urbana-Champaign. Her research has two interrelated goals: one, to understand how normal cognitive aging and age-related conditions (e.g., mild cognitive impairment, Alzheimer's dementia, age-associated hearing loss) impact cognitive and social health; and two, to develop nonpharmacological interventions to support cognitive and social health in older adults. Mudar has served as the co-chair of the Joint Committee on Interprofessional Relations Between the American Psychological Association and the American Speech-Language-Hearing Association (ASHA) and is an ASHA Fellow. Her research is funded by the National Institutes of Health through the National Institute of Nursing Research. Mudar has a Ph.D. in communication sciences and disorders from the University of Texas at Dallas.

FRANK OSWALD (he /him/his) is professor for interdisciplinary ageing research, chair of the Frankfurt Forum for interdisciplinary Ageing Research at the Goethe University, Germany, and director of the Goethe Research Academy for Early Career Researchers Center for Aging. His research interests include contexts of adult development, issues of person-environment transaction and transitions in old age, housing, ageing in place, relocation, and the role of technologies in later life. Oswald has conducted research in the field of environmental gerontology on the local, national, and European level. He is a fellow of the Gerontological Society of America, a member of the International Society for Gerontechnology, and of the International Association for People-Environment Studies. Oswald's research is funded by the European Commission, the German Research Foundation, several federal German ministries, communities, and private foundations (e.g., the Volkswagen Foundation). He has a Ph.D. in psychology from the University Heidelberg.

MANISH N. SHAH (he/him/his) is professor and chair of the BerbeeWalsh Department of Emergency Medicine at the University of Wisconsin–Madison and holds the Azita G. Hamedani Distinguished Chair of Emergency Medicine. As a practicing emergency medicine physician and a researcher with funding from the National Institutes of Health, the Agency for Healthcare Research and Quality, Centers for Disease Control and Prevention, and the Health Resources and Services Administration, Shah has dedicated his career to improving the care delivered to acutely ill or injured older adults. His work has helped establish the field of geriatric emergency medicine and advanced the role of ambulance-based paramedics to support community health efforts, now termed "community paramedicine." Shah's recent work, which has taken place in both urban and rural communities in Wisconsin and New York, has focused on helping persons living with dementia. He has received the Paul B. Beeson Career Development Award from the National Institute on Aging and the Pioneer Award from the Academy of Geriatric Emergency Medicine. Shah completed his residency in emergency medicine at The Ohio State University and further research training through the Robert Wood Johnson Clinical Scholars Program. He received a bachelor's degree from the University of Chicago and an M.D. and M.P.H. from the University of Rochester.

REGINA SHIH (she/her/hers) is a professor of epidemiology at Emory University's Rollins School of Public Health, adjunct senior policy researcher at RAND, and board member of the National Alliance for Caregiving. Dr. Shih's diverse research interests are centered on community-engaged approaches and policy-relevant outcomes achieved through multilevel analysis of large datasets, study design, strategic planning, and program evaluation. With collaborators, she is estimating the long-term effects of redlining on older adult cognitive health, modeling the social networks of dementia family caregivers, engaging villages to promote healthy aging interventions, and advancing dementia home- and community-based services research through the Community Care Network for Dementia (CaN-D). Previously she led projects that examined neighborhood influences on dementia risk, published a policy blueprint for dementia long-term care that resulted in Congressional testimony; and developed a toolkit for public health departments and age-friendly initiatives to collaborate on older adult climate preparedness. She holds a B.A. in neuroscience from the Johns Hopkins University and a Ph.D. in psychiatric epidemiology from the Johns Hopkins Bloomberg School of Public Health.

LAURA TREJO (she/her/hers), the director of the Los Angeles County Aging and Disabilities Department, is responsible for launching a new county department along with establishing a proactive, coordinated, and comprehensive strategy and service delivery system for older adults and adults with disabilities. She oversees programs and operations such as Adult Protective Services, the Area Agency on Aging, 14 Community and Senior Centers, and the work of the Los Angeles Commission on Older Adults and Commission on Disabilities. Trejo was general manager of the City of Los Angeles Department of Aging and the first district chief for countywide older adult mental health for the Los Angeles County Department of Mental Health. A national leader and trailblazer, she has consulted with and trained other leaders throughout the United States on the development of programs for older adults, focusing on cultural competence. An internationally recognized expert, Trejo has worked with international organizations and countries around the world to develop initiatives and programs in the areas of aging, mental health, Alzheimer's, and rehabilitation. She currently serves as president of the California Association of Area Agencies on Aging and serves on various boards and committees, including the editorial board of *Generations*. Trejo has received numerous awards for excellence and leadership, among them the Robert Wood Johnson Foundation's Community Health Leadership Award. She holds an M.S. in gerontology, an M.P.A., a graduate certificate in long term-care administration, and a Ph.D. in social work, all from the University of Southern California.